D0288558

THE
BIBLE
IN ENGLISH
TRANSLATION

Abingdon Essential Guides
Editorial Advisory Board

Nancy T. Ammerman
Hartford Seminary

Don S. Browning
University of Chicago Divinity School

Rebecca S. Chopp
Candler School of Theology

Justo L. González
Emory University

Walter J. Harrelson
Vanderbilt University Divinity School

E. Brooks Holifield
Candler School of Theology

George G. Hunter
Asbury Theological Seminary

Allan Kirton
The United Methodist Mission Resource Center

Jane Dammen McAuliffe
University of Toronto

Peter J. Paris
Princeton Theological Seminary

Orlo Strunk, Jr.
The Journal of Pastoral Care

THE BIBLE IN ENGLISH TRANSLATION

An ESSENTIAL GUIDE

Steven M. Sheeley
Robert N. Nash, Jr.

ABINGDON PRESS
Nashville

THE BIBLE IN ENGLISH TRANSLATION:
AN ESSENTIAL GUIDE

Copyright © 1997 by Abingdon Press

All Rights Reserved.

No part of this work may be reproduced or transmitted in any form or
by any means, electronic or mechanical, including photocopying and
recording, or by any information storage or retrieval system, except as
may be expressly permitted by the 1976 Copyright Act or in writing from
the publisher. Requests for permission should be addressed in writing
to Abingdon Press, 201 Eighth Avenue South, P. O. Box 801, Nashville,
TN 37202, U.S.A.

This book is printed on acid-free, recycled paper.

Library of Congress Cataloging-in-Publication Data

Sheeley, Steven M.
    The Bible in English translation: an essential guide / Steven M.
Sheeley
        p.   cm.
    Includes bibliographical references
    ISBN 0-687-001536 (alk. paper)
    1. Bible—History. 2. Bible. English—Versions. I. Nash, Robert
N. II. Title.
BS445.S44 1997
220.5′2′009—dc21   97-31594
                                                                     CIP

97 98 99 00 01 02 03 04 05 06 — 10 9 8 7 6 5 4 3 2 1

MANUFACTURED IN THE UNITED STATES OF AMERICA

To our students

Contents

Acknowledgments

This book has been much more than simply a joint effort between two authors. In many ways, it reflects the intersection between our lives and the lives of numerous people who have influenced our love and appreciation for the Bible. Parents and grandparents, Sunday school teachers, ministers, aunts and uncles, and friends all must be included in such a list. These people have been fully grounded in the Bible, and their love for it has been a wonderful example to us of the ways in which the Scriptures can bring purpose to human lives.

Our home churches, the North Broad Baptist Church and the First Baptist Church, both located in Rome, Georgia, offer us communities of faith in which to live out biblical truth. We are grateful for these Christians who constantly challenge us toward higher ground.

We owe a special debt of gratitude to our teachers at both The Southern Baptist Theological Seminary and the Southwestern Baptist Theological Seminary in the decade between 1979 and 1989. Persons such as R. Alan Culpepper, James Brooks, Bruce Corley, Bill J. Leonard, John Polhill, E. Glenn Hinson, and Marvin Tate combined the best of critical scholarship and warm hearted faith with a love for the Bible. Their lives are sufficient evidence for us of its truth.

A word of thanks must be extended to a number of people at Shorter College. Stephanie McFarland and Melanie Register, our student assistants in the 1995–97 school years, helped with bibliographical information, photocopying, and a number of other essential tasks. Kim Herndon, Karen Simpkins, and other staff librarians at the Livingston Library assisted with research and with securing interlibrary loan materials. The Professional Development Committee of the faculty along with Provost Harold Newman provided some timely financial support for the project.

Finally, we owe an enormous debt to Elizabeth and Guyeth, Kristen, Lindsay, Mary, and Douglas for the weekends and nights that we spent at the office rather than at home and for their love and support. We hope that this book can be a valuable tool, especially for our children, as their love for the Bible deepens.

Shorter Hill
Rome, Georgia
Easter 1997

Chapter 1

The Making of the English Bible

All he wanted to do was to buy a Bible!

"Which translation do you prefer?" asked the helpful sales-clerk. "We have NIVs, NASBs, KJVs, NKJVs, JBs, RSVs, NRSVs, NABs. You name it and we have it!"

"Uh, okay! Let me look at the NIV and the King James."

She smiled. "Which King James? Old King James or New King James?"

"You're kidding me!" he exclaimed.

She shook her head and led him toward the shelves. Bibles of every shape and color took up an entire bookcase in the religion section.

"Let's see," she intoned, as her eyes scanned the shelves. "In the King James we've got a Life Application Bible, a Full Life Study Bible, a Rainbow Children's Bible, the Original African Heritage Bible, and the One Year Bible. In the New King James we have this Young Explorer's Bible, a Life Application Bible for Students, a Precious Moments Bible, a Spirit-Filled Life Study Bible, and a Word in Life Bible."

She took a breath. "And, in the NIV we have both a Men's and Women's Devotional Bible, an NIV Study Bible, a Student Bible, and a New Adventure Bible for kids."

"Will one of these do, sir? Or would you like to look at options in other translations?"

"I just wanted a Bible," he muttered to himself.

Choosing a Bible these days is certainly not easy! The dizzying array of translations and specialty Bibles directed at everyone from athletes to executives to teenagers is both blessing and curse. The good news? There is a Bible for you. The bad news? Good luck in finding it!

How can you make an educated decision when it comes to selecting a Bible? Do you know how the Bible came to be in its present form? When was it first translated into English? How can you be sure that the English Bible you hold in your hands is a faithful translation of the text in the original languages of the biblical writers? What is to keep someone from changing a word here or there or adding a marginal note to shore up a particular theological position? Should you simply trust the translators? Or should you make some effort to understand the processes and philosophies that guided these translations in order to choose one that is suitable for you?

The answers to these questions are obvious to us. The Bible is our guide for faith and a major source of our theology and practice. It is much too important a book to be lifted blindly from a bookstore shelf without giving any thought to how it got there in the first place.

So we have written this book as your guide to the English Bible. Here we have traced the process by which the books of the Bible were first joined together into a common collection or canon. We have followed that common collection through Christian history as it was translated into the English language, often at a terrible price. We have summarized the translation process, describing the various philosophies of translation and decisions about manuscripts that lie beneath each of the major English versions of the Bible. And finally, we have categorized the various versions and offered some practical advice to help you in choosing and using an appropriate translation.

How the Bible Came to Be

The Bible didn't just appear on a bookstore shelf complete with leather binding and gold lettering. The journey of the Bible to that shelf is a fascinating story, full of twists and turns. The word *Bible* comes from the Greek word *biblion* which means "little book" or "papyrus," a reference to the plant from which the earliest writing paper was made. The plural form of *biblion* is *biblios*, meaning "little books."

Indeed, the Bible is a collection of "little books" that were written over a period of some 1,100 years. This collection is divided into two testaments, the Old Testament (or Jewish Scriptures), which relates the history and faith of Israel, and the New Testament, which contains the life and teachings of Jesus and relates the story of the emergence of Christianity.

The Old Testament

The Old Testament portion of the Bible emerged centuries ago out of the oral traditions of Judaism, as stories of God's relationship to Israel were passed down from generation to generation. These stories were eventually written onto scrolls and collected for permanent safekeeping. Later, the *oracles* (or sayings) of the prophets of Israel and other kinds of history and wisdom literature were also preserved.

Through a process called *canonization*, the Jewish people determined which books should be considered "sacred" writings and which books should not. The word *canon* means "an authoritative list for a given community." The books or collections that made the Jewish "list" of sacred writings were those books to which the faithful turned most often for spiritual encouragement. These books were eventually gathered together into a single collection called the Hebrew Scriptures or, for Christians, the Old Testament.

The canonization of the Old Testament was a lengthy process that took many centuries. Certain books or scrolls came to have special meaning for the people of Israel. These books offered hope to a people who often found themselves in the midst of political upheaval and social instability. Over time, certain books came to be read and reread in the synagogues as sources of encouragement for living and hope for the future messianic age.

The Hebrew Scriptures that were finally accepted into the canon can be divided into three categories: the Law (or Torah), the Prophets, and the Writings.

The Law. The Law (Torah), which includes the first five books of the Bible (Genesis to Deuteronomy), contains the oldest stories of God's relationship to Israel. These stories first circulated as oral tradition in Israel before taking written form about 1000 B.C.E. The written accounts were then used as source materials by an editor or editors who fashioned the first permanent record of the history of Israel's relationship to God. This record contains the central Jewish stories of the creation, of Israel's matriarchs and patriarchs, of God's covenant with Abraham, and of the Exodus from Egypt. It also contains hundreds of laws that governed every aspect of Jewish life.

13

These books of the Law were generally accepted as the foundation of Jewish faith about 400 B.C.E., shortly after the return of the Jewish exiles to Palestine from Babylon.

The Prophets. The prophetic literature of the Old Testament includes both historical books and oracles by particular prophets of Israel. These books are divided into the two categories of the Former and the Latter Prophets. The Former Prophets include the historical books of Joshua, Judges, Samuel, and Kings. The Latter Prophets consist of oracles pronounced by Isaiah, Jeremiah, Ezekiel (also known as the Major Prophets because of the length of their books), and the Minor Prophets of Hosea through Malachi (also known as the Book of the Twelve). All of these writings were generally accepted as sacred by about 200 B.C.E.

The Writings. The Writings were the last category to be widely accepted as sacred Jewish literature, being finally adopted about 90 C.E. when the Jewish canon was closed. They are a diverse collection of wisdom literature, proverbs, histories, and stories and include books such as Psalms, Proverbs, Job, Ruth, Ecclesiastes, Esther, Lamentations, Song of Songs, Daniel, Chronicles, Ezra, and Nehemiah.

The Closing of the Old Testament Canon

Jewish religious authorities became concerned about preserving the Jewish faith after the destruction of Jerusalem by the Romans in 70 C.E. Central to this discussion was the debate over which books should be included in the Jewish canon so as to maintain a "fixed" source for the story of God's relationship and covenant with Israel. These authorities hoped that a canonical list of sacred writings would allow Jews to maintain their faith even as they dispersed all over the Mediterranean basin.

A rabbinic academy, established at Jamnia on the Mediterranean Sea, became the focus for this debate. There, about 90 C.E., decisions were made about which of the Writings would be added to the Law and the Prophets. The Jewish canon was then closed. The entire process of canonization from the time of the earliest writings to the adoption of the final sacred books at Jamnia had taken approximately one thousand years.

The New Testament

The New Testament emerged from the oral traditions about Jesus that developed after his death and resurrection. The disciples and others who witnessed Jesus' ministry recounted the events of his life to the earliest Christian converts. About 45–50 C.E., the apostle Paul penned his first letter to the church at Thessalonica. Biblical scholars believe this letter to be the oldest surviving New Testament writing.

Other letters, including the second letter to Thessalonica, the personal letter to Philemon, and those to the churches of Corinth, Rome, Galatia, Philippi, Colossae, and Ephesus, followed in rapid succession until Paul's death around 65 C.E. These letters were generally accepted as sacred literature, collected, and circulated among the various churches as the first Christian Scriptures.

The eventual deaths of eyewitnesses to Jesus' life and ministry probably compelled the church to put the stories of his life into written form. The Gospel of Mark was the first such account to be written, probably between 65 and 70 C.E. The Gospels of Matthew and Luke followed some fifteen to twenty years later. Each Gospel presents a unique theological perspective on the ministry of Jesus. Matthew and Luke probably used Mark as a major source.

Luke's gospel is the first volume of a two-volume series that concludes with the Acts of the Apostles, composed shortly after its companion gospel. The Gospel of John, probably written between 90 and 100 C.E., interprets Jesus' ministry in highly spiritualized language that distinguishes it from the other Gospels.

The remaining books of the New Testament, including the Pastoral Epistles of 1 and 2 Timothy and Titus, the general Epistles of James, Peter, John, and Jude, and the books of Hebrews and Revelation, were written either late in the first century or early in the second century C.E. Some scholars have proposed a date as early as 65 C.E. for Hebrews and as late as 150 C.E. for 2 Peter. Christians of the first three centuries only gradually recognized these books as sacred, while granting almost universal authority to the Gospels, Acts, and Paul's epistles.

The Canon of the New Testament

For three full centuries, the books listed above circulated among Christian congregations alongside numerous other gospels, letters, and theological treatises. Christians spent much of this period in a defensive posture, battling external threats in the form of persecution by the Roman Empire and internal threats brought about by theological disputes over orthodoxy and heresy. During this period, the Jewish Bible, the Gospels, and Paul's epistles were generally recognized as "Scripture."

Two major internal challenges to Christianity in the second century convinced church leaders of the need for an authoritative list of acceptable sacred works. Marcion, a Gnostic Christian in Rome, believed that the God of the Jewish Scriptures was an evil God who had created an imperfect world. Marcion rejected the entire canon of the Old Testament because it celebrated the accomplishments of this evil God. He accepted as sacred Scripture only the Gospel of Luke and Paul's epistles, which he believed to tell the story of the good God of Jesus Christ who had redeemed the world from the clutches of the evil God.

Montanus, a native of western Asia Minor, attracted considerable attention in 172 C.E. when he proclaimed himself the mouthpiece of the Holy Spirit. Montanists placed equal weight upon the authority of Scripture and the immediate inspiration of the Spirit in an individual. They challenged the complacency of the church with a call for radical separation from the world and even encouraged martyrdom.

The rapid growth of Marcionism and Montanism alarmed church leaders and moved the church another step toward a fixed New Testament canon that would protect Christians from unorthodox theological interpretations. The Muratorian canon, proposed in the late second century, included some writings that would be accepted into the final canon (the Gospels and Acts, Paul's epistles, Jude, 1 and 2 John, and Revelation) and some that would not be accepted (Wisdom of Solomon and the Apocalypse of Peter).

Other lists were proposed by Origen and Eusebius in the third century. Origen, born in Alexandria, Egypt, was a prolific author and respected theologian/philosopher who used Platonic philosophy to explain the Christian faith. His criteria for a book's inclusion in the canon were dependent upon how widely it was used by the churches. He included the four Gospels, Acts, Paul's epistles, 1 Peter, 1 John, and Revelation. He harbored doubts about the books of Hebrews, James, 2 Peter, 2 and 3 John, and other apocryphal works.

Eusebius, Bishop of Caesarea and the first historian of the church, suggested the same books except that he probably added Hebrews

16

to the list and admitted that James, 2 Peter, 2 and 3 John, and Jude were considered sacred by many churches.

The Closing of the New Testament Canon

The first definitive listing of the twenty-seven books of the New Testament came in 367 C.E. in the Easter Letter written by Athanasius, the Bishop of Alexandria, in Egypt. This same list was officially approved some thirty years later at a general council of the church held at Carthage. The process of canonization of the New Testament lasted almost four hundred years, from the writing of 1 Thessalonians in the mid first century to the early years of the fifth century.

Early Translations

Translations of both the Old and New Testaments were first undertaken in order to make the Scriptures available to wider audiences.

The Septuagint. The Jewish Scriptures were translated into Greek from Hebrew and Aramaic in the third century B.C.E. This translation, known as the Septuagint, took about two centuries to complete and was intended for Jewish audiences outside of Palestine who did not speak Hebrew. Early Christians used this Greek translation of the Hebrew Scriptures as their Bible.

Included in the Septuagint were a number of Jewish writings which were later referred to as apocryphal or "hidden" writings. These writings were thought to contain secret or coded messages for the faithful. The seven books of the Apocrypha, along with additions to the books of Esther and Daniel, were to be read privately but were not intended for public worship. Jewish officials rejected the books of the Apocrypha from the Jewish canon during their deliberations in Jamnia.

The Vulgate. The entire Bible was translated into Latin from the original languages in the late fourth century C.E. by Jerome, a native of Italy and a high church official. Jerome traveled extensively in Egypt and Palestine before settling down in Bethlehem to complete his translation. It was officially commissioned by the Bishop of Rome and, because Latin was the language of the common (or "vulgar") people, became known as the Vulgate.

Jerome included in this translation only those New Testament books that Athanasius had listed in his Easter Letter. Like the Septuagint, the Vulgate also contained the books of the Apocrypha as part of the Old Testament. Jerome's translation was widely accepted by the church, thus effectively closing the biblical canon.

The Three Canons

Slight differences exist between the canons of Judaism, Catholicism, and Protestantism. The Jewish canon includes only the twenty-four books of the Jewish Scriptures. This number differs from the thirty-nine books of the Old Testament because the Jewish Scriptures do not divide the books of Kings, Numbers, and Chronicles; combine Ezra and Nehemiah; and consider the twelve Minor Prophets to be a single book.

The Catholic or Christian canon consists of the thirty-nine books of the Old Testament, the twenty-seven books of the New Testament, and seven additional books from the Apocrypha, including Tobit, Judith, the Wisdom of Solomon, Ecclesiasticus, Baruch, 1 and 2 Maccabees, and additions to Esther and Daniel. These books were officially added at the Council of Trent in 1546 in the aftermath of the Protestant Reformation.

The Protestant canon recognizes only the thirty-nine books of the Old Testament and the twenty-seven books of the New Testament. It rejects the Apocrypha primarily because the Jewish canon also rejected it. It also organizes the books of the Old Testament in a format slightly different from that of the Jewish Scriptures.

The History of the English Bible

Jerome's Vulgate served as the official Bible of the church for almost one thousand years. Its place remained unchallenged even as classical Latin ceased to be a spoken language. In time, only the educated clergy could read and interpret it. A small number of English translations were undertaken prior to the fourteenth century. Venerable Bede, an English monk, translated portions of the Vulgate into English in the eighth century, but no copies of his work have survived. Various sections of the Bible were also translated into English in the eleventh and twelfth centuries.

John Wycliffe, an English priest and church reformer of the fourteenth century, is responsible for the first full translation of the

Bible into English. He believed that the Bible belonged in the hands of the common people of Europe, and particularly of England. After his death in 1384, his followers completed his translation of the Latin Vulgate. The Wycliffe Bible was condemned by the church in 1408 out of fear that erroneous interpretations might result if the Bible became available in the popular languages of Europe. The church banned all such translation efforts.

The invention of the printing press in 1455 by Johannes Gutenberg resulted in the spread of common language translations of the Bible across Europe. Martin Luther, the great Protestant reformer, published a German version in 1522 ,which was translated from the original languages of Greek, Hebrew, and Aramaic.

William Tyndale followed Luther's lead in 1525 with an English version of the New Testament translated from the Greek text and greatly influenced by Luther's German translation. Tyndale, a graduate of Oxford and tutor to the family of an English noble, has been called the "Father of the English Bible." He fled to Germany to publish his New Testament when it became clear that the church in England would not allow an English translation. He later added the first five books of the Old Testament and Jonah to his English translation.

In 1535 he was arrested near Brussels, convicted of treason for ignoring the prohibitions against common language translations, and executed the next year. Other portions of the Old Testament were translated by his followers shortly after his death. Nearly every English translation for the next two hundred years borrowed extensively from Tyndale's work, including the King James Bible of 1611.

Sixteenth- and Seventeenth-Century English Translations

After 1530, political and religious conflicts in England often influenced efforts to publish new translations of the Bible. For most of the seventeenth century, England was embroiled in a crisis over the religious direction of the nation. The throne passed back and forth between Protestant and Catholic monarchs; first Catholics and then Protestants were forced to flee to the European continent. Both groups undertook new translations of the Bible in order to protect the faithful from erroneous interpretations by the other.

At the same time, Calvinist theology was imported into England by dissenters who had fled to John Calvin's Geneva to escape Catho-

19

lic persecution. Protestants were often divided over Calvin's views, particularly his ideas regarding predestination. Many were suspicious of any translation that contained marginal notes with heavily Calvinistic leanings. Some translations supported Calvinist interpretations while others refuted it.

The Coverdale Bible (1535). Tyndale's student, Myles Coverdale, published an English translation of the Latin Vulgate and Luther's German Bible in 1535. It received a royal license from King Henry VIII and was widely disseminated across England.

Matthew's Bible (1537). John Rogers, another of Tyndale's followers, published Matthew's Bible in 1537, using the pseudonym of Thomas Matthew. This translation was essentially Tyndale's translation with the addition of those Old Testament books that had been left untranslated at Tyndale's untimely death.

The Great Bible (1539). Concerns quickly arose about the heavily Protestant flavor of both The Coverdale Bible and Matthew's Bible. In 1538 Thomas Cranmer, Archbishop of Canterbury, called for a new translation that would correct this bias. Myles Coverdale revised Matthew's Bible in 1539 and republished it as The Great Bible. Copies were placed in every church in England.

The Geneva Bible (1560) and **The Bishop's Bible (1568).** Two highly popular English Bibles were translated in the mid–sixteenth century. The Geneva Bible, translated by William Whittingham and published in Geneva in 1560, was quite popular in Elizabethan England because of its obvious Protestant leanings. A revision of The Great Bible, this version was translated from the original languages. The Bishop's Bible was published in 1568 by those leaders of the Church of England who could not tolerate the intense Calvinist leanings of The Geneva Bible.

The Douay-Rheims Bible (1609). An English Catholic Bible was translated by Catholic exiles in France during the reign of Queen Elizabeth I. Gregory Martin completed this entire translation of the Latin Vulgate, publishing the New Testament at Rheims in 1582 and the Old Testament at Douay in 1609–10. Revised by Richard Challoner in 1749, the Douay Bible served as the official English Bible of the Catholic church until a second Catholic translation was published by Ronald A. Knox in the 1940s.

The King James Bible (1611). Dissatisfaction with the heavily Calvinist leanings of The Geneva Bible lasted well into the seventeenth century. In 1604 Puritan clergymen convinced King James I of the need for a new translation that would be free of interpretative marginal notes. James himself had voiced disagreement with notes in The Geneva Bible, which he believed to interfere with the notion of the divine right of kings.

Work on the new translation was divided among fifty-four renowned translators from the universities of Oxford, Cambridge, and Westminster. These translators were divided into six teams, each responsible for translating a section of the Old and New Testaments and the Apocrypha. The work of each team was carefully reviewed by other teams, and the final translation was edited by two representatives from each team.

Several guidelines were adopted by the translation committee. The Bishop's Bible was to provide overall direction for the translation. Also, proper names were to be translated according to popular usage in the seventeenth century. Marginal notes were used only when necessary to clarify Greek and Hebrew words or to point out parallel texts. The lack of marginal notes was intended to produce a translation that would finally be acceptable across the theological spectrum.

The influence of the King James Version, or Authorized Version as it came to be called, cannot be exaggerated. Within a few years after its publication in 1611, it had replaced previous translations as the English Bible of choice to be read in both the local parish and at home. It stands as one of the outstanding masterpieces of the English language. Various editions were published between 1613 and 1769, when an official revision was finally adopted. The Revised Version was published in England in 1885 and in the United States in 1901 where it was known as the American Standard Version. The King James Version (KJV) continues to be widely read today.

Conclusion

The KJV provided a common Bible for English Protestantism well into the twentieth century. However, as time passed, new Greek and Hebrew manuscripts were discovered that were often much older than the manuscripts available to translators in the seventeenth century. These older manuscripts exposed errors in the manuscripts upon which the KJV was based. In addition, they now complicate the task of biblical scholars who are forced to choose from a number of manuscripts before undertaking a new translation. In the following chapter we will learn about these new manuscripts and the unique challenges of Bible translation in our own day.

Suggested Readings

Bruce, F. F. *History of the Bible in English*. New York: Oxford University Press, 1978.

Lewis, Jack P. *The English Bible from KJV to NIV: A History and Evaluation*. Grand Rapids: Baker Book House, 1981.

CHAPTER 2

Translating the Bible

I t's all 'Greek' to me," is the running joke in New Testament Greek classes everywhere, whether in college or seminary. This excuse helps to cover the nervousness of students at the challenge of learning a new and unfamiliar language. Most of us never face the great unknown of studying the Greek and Hebrew languages. We have grown so accustomed to having the Bible in our native language that we fail to appreciate those who have devoted their lives to translating the words of Scripture from ancient Hebrew and Greek texts into English. We turn now to their work of translation, hoping that a better understanding of the process of translation will aid our analysis and evaluation of the translations now available.

Although the process of translation is actually not very easy to divide into sections, this chapter will do just that, separating our discussion of translating the Bible into the following sections: text and context. In reality, both of these sections address tasks that the translator must keep together as she or he works to bridge the gap between the ancient and the modern languages. Here lies the purpose of the entire enterprise; it is an attempt to transform the words of an ancient culture into the words of our modern English-speaking culture.

The Text of the Bible

The first task of the translator is to decide what those ancient words were. It seems so simple from our perspective; all the words of the Bible have been gathered together and published. What we do not see, though, is the work that preceded the publication of both the Hebrew Bible and the Greek New Testament. We need to go back in time long enough to see the words of the Bible before they were gathered together into published volumes, to see them in their previous lives as parts of scrolls and texts. Once there, we realize that each text is slightly different from its neighbor. Texts can change from generation to generation as they are copied by hand, and the inadvertent mistakes of one copier can find their way into future copies, becoming part of Scripture itself.

The problem is compounded by the number of manuscripts available. If we possessed the original manuscripts of both the Old and New Testaments (called *autographs*), we could know with certainty where to begin the process of translation. But those manuscripts have been lost or destroyed and are no longer available. In their place we have thousands of manuscripts, of various ages, and they offer us hundreds of thousands of slightly different ways to read the biblical text. That many of them exist at all borders on the miraculous, since they were written with ink on *papyrus*, an early form of paper made with layered stalks of the papyrus plant. Other ancient manuscripts are slightly more durable, written on *vellum* or *parchment*, the scraped, washed, and prepared skin of a goat or other animal.

By the time of the New Testament, the Hebrew text had reached a written form very similar to the text that exists today. Much of this is due to the work of a group of scholars called *masoretes*, so the resulting text of the Hebrew Bible is known as the Masoretic Text (MT). The earliest New Testament texts were produced in the second, third, and fourth centuries C.E. Roughly one-third of them are papyrus texts; the others survive on parchment. These manuscripts were written using capital Greek letters (or *uncials*). Apparently, around the beginning of the ninth century a new method of writing Greek came into use, and the manuscripts produced after this time used lowercase letters (called *minuscules*). Evidence for the text of the New Testament has also been preserved in Greek *lectionaries* (used for worship and devotion) and quotations of the New Testament by the early church fathers.

Enter the "textual critic." While everyone who prepares for serious academic study of the Hebrew Bible and the New Testament has some knowledge of textual criticism, a few biblical scholars specialize in this field. They pore over the ancient texts and determine which words ought to have a place in the resulting "final" text. They analyze and categorize the various readings of the ancient texts, working with thoroughness and precision.

The result is a number of published texts of the Hebrew Bible and Greek New Testament that are generally accepted among the scholarly community. These texts provide a starting point for the rest of the translation process. Textual critics fashion ancient texts that are as close to the original biblical texts as possible given the resources available.

The Context of the Bible: Then and Now

Textual criticism is only the first step in the process of translating the Bible into English. At its heart lies the need to translate not only the ancient words but the ancient culture as well. A successful modern translation must bridge the gap between the ancient and the modern worlds. This task raises philosophical questions that a translator (or editorial board) must answer before work can begin. Do we try to reproduce the ancient words themselves, translated into their modern equivalents? Or do we attempt to reproduce the thoughts and ideas of the ancient text, translated into their modern equivalents? How will this philosophical decision affect the translation? How much responsibility does the translator bear for bridging the cultural and historical gap between the modern reader and the ancient author or editor?

Modern English translations of the Bible can be divided along the lines of how these questions have been answered. On one end of the spectrum are those versions that attempt to reproduce the modern English equivalent of the ancient word. Such versions are termed *verbal* translations. On the other end of the spectrum are those versions that are more concerned to reproduce the ancient thoughts and ideas in their modern English equivalents. To this end, verbal equivalence is often sacrificed in order to translate the meaning of the ancient language as faithfully as possible. Such versions are called *dynamic* translations.

Paraphrase is a third category of versions. Sometimes the boundary between a paraphrase and a dynamic translation is unclear. While a dynamic translation involves some paraphrasing (since the ancient words must be rewritten in the language and words of the modern translator and reader in order to convey with accuracy the meaning of the ancient text), the paraphrased version attempts to update the language of a previous English translation. The verbal and dynamic translations begin with the ancient texts and their words; the paraphrase usually makes little reference to the ancient texts. The resulting version is popular and easy to read, but it runs the risk of losing its connection with the biblical text itself.

The Verbal Translations

Probably the best-known translation in this category is the King James Version, published in 1611. Drawing on the textual and translation work of people such as John Wycliffe and William Tyndale, a group of biblical scholars in England were assembled at the instigation of James I to translate the entire Bible into English. Their assignment was to produce a translation "as consonant as can be to the original Hebrew and Greek." Subsequent versions, such as the Revised Version and New English Bible/Revised English Bible (in England) and the Revised Standard Version, New American Standard Bible, New International Version, New King James Version, and the New Revised Standard Version (in the United States), have attempted to update the language of the translation while maintaining its philosophy.

These translations are often radically different from one another. Some of this difference comes from the strictness with which the translators applied their philosophy. Does the need to reproduce a verbal equivalence extend to the order of the words within each sentence? The translators of the New American Standard Bible (NASB) made every effort to maintain the word order of the ancient text in their translation. Does verbal equivalence demand that each occurrence of the ancient word be translated into the same English word? The translators disagree, and their translations reflect that disagreement. Such questions, and the answers given by translators and editors of different versions, provide a basis for comparison between modern English translations, even within a general philosophical category. That comparison will be the subject of later chapters in this book.

The Dynamic Translations

While the KJV became the Bible of much of the English-speaking world, biblical scholars and Bible readers continued to explore the possibilities for translating the ancient texts into their own modern English language. As the English language changed, some readers of the Bible demanded that the language of their Bible develop as well. In addition, missionaries and others were working diligently to translate the Bible into other languages. Their experiences also informed the philosophy of translation into English. Speakers of modern, often colloquial, English wanted a Bible in which the characters spoke their language rather than the language of Shakespeare. Translators and missionaries were more interested in proclaiming the gospel message in a form that non-Christians could understand than they were in preserving the words and word order of the ancient texts.

Probably the most popular dynamic translation is the Good News Bible or Today's English Version (GNB/TEV). Translated and published by and for the American Bible Society, this version presented the content of the Bible in the language of the modern English-speaking world. More than that, the GNB/TEV presented the Bible's contents in the language and the form of the 1970s. Such a realization raises an interesting point about the dynamic versions. They quickly become dated when the modern colloquial language changes. Their popularity diminishes. Realizing that limitation, the American Bible Society has recently released The Contemporary English Version, a translation of the Bible's contents into the language and forms of the English-speaking world of the 1990s.

Another significant example of a dynamic translation is the Jerusalem Bible (JB). One thing that sets the JB apart from other dynamic translations is its intention not only to translate the ancient ideas into modern language, but to do so within a Roman Catholic context. J. B. Phillips was similarly motivated by his perception that the young people in war-torn London needed a translation of the New Testament that they could read in their own language, so he published The New Testament in Modern English. The translation of the New Testament that bears his name became his life's work and a lasting contribution to the translation of the Bible into English. Phillips recognized the need to continue to revise the dynamic translation to keep pace with the changing forms of modern English.

While the differences in translation between dynamic versions are more easily explained than those in the verbal translation category, such differences still raise questions. Here, though, the questions are more likely to relate to the translator's conception of modern English. What idiomatic or colloquial expression best captures the meaning of the ancient passage? How true to the ancient language and its images must a dynamic translation be? Will updating the image change the meaning of the text entirely? How modern can the translation afford to be and still survive as an effective tool for communicating the biblical message? These and other questions will be posed to different dynamic translations later in this book.

The Paraphrase

As we mentioned earlier, making a clear distinction between the dynamic translation and the paraphrase is difficult. The very process of translation from one language into another will involve a certain measure of paraphrase. This is especially true of the Bible, since the biblical languages have a form and rhythm that do not always lend themselves to exact reproduction in English. In addition, the biblical languages were living languages (that is, people were still speaking and writing them when the Bible was being written); both Hebrew and Greek changed during the time the Testaments were being written, as did their colloquial and idiomatic expressions. Some of those idioms will not translate easily into an English equivalent. When that is the case, even verbal translations are forced to look for a functional rather than a literal English equivalent, and that translation will involve a paraphrase.

A paraphrased version usually begins with an existing English translation. Rather than producing a new translation from the ancient languages, the paraphrase is intended only to update another modern language version. Often this intention springs from the recognition that modern language and culture are changing, and people are unable to grasp the meaning of the Scripture because that meaning is obscured by the language difference. Despite the KJV's dominance in the English-speaking world, many have defended paraphrases by citing the increasing gap between the language of Elizabethan England and that of twentieth-century America. That gap, they claim, demonstrates a need for a version of the Bible that modern readers can easily understand.

As you can see, the argument for a paraphrased version differs little from that put forward for new dynamic and verbal translations. The main difference between the paraphrase and other types of modern English versions is the starting place. Where the verbal and dynamic translations seek to bridge the gap between the modern reader and the ancient writer, the paraphrase seeks to bridge the gap between a modern translation and an even more modern reader. By devoting less attention to the ancient texts, the paraphrase runs the risk of interpreting the modern translation rather than the ancient texts. With this interpretation comes the risk that the paraphraser will inject his or her theological bias into the text itself. This is not to say that a certain amount of theological bias is not present in every translation. After all, every translator must choose which English word best represents the ancient word, and such choices will always involve a certain amount of bias. The paraphraser, though, may choose not only to update the language of other modern versions, but to emphasize or advocate certain theological positions, as well. The danger of a translator's commentary becoming part of the text itself has always been present in the process of translation, but the danger increases with a paraphrase.

One particular paraphrase captured the attention of the American religious public in the 1970s and 1980s. *The Living Bible* was published in a time when record numbers of Americans were returning to the Bible and to church. Since they had left the Bible and the church in part because of their difficulty in understanding and feeling comfortable with the traditional nature of the Bible and church, the LB spoke to their need for a more contemporary Bible. The LB seemed to breathe life into what had become for many a "dead" Bible. Its language was contemporary and fresh, communicating the words of Jesus and Paul in exciting new ways. More recently, *The Message*, a paraphrase by Eugene Peterson, has caught the imagination of a new generation of Americans seeking to understand the Bible.

These and other paraphrases will be examined more closely in a later chapter on dynamic translations and paraphrases.

Conclusion

Many who read, study, and use the Bible daily are bewildered by the range of choices that confronts them when they try to choose a Bible. The sheer number of translations is overwhelming, not to mention the need to decide which set of notes and commentary to buy with that translation. What should be a simple decision is turned into a difficult one.

We have surveyed the processes and philosophies of translating the Bible for two reasons. First, this survey provides a framework for the rest of this book. Future chapters of this book will divide our analysis and evaluation of the modern English translations on the basis of the philosophy they most seem to follow. Chapter 3 will discuss the most significant verbal translations. Chapter 4 will consider dynamic translations and the paraphrases.

Our review of the problems associated with translating the words of ancient texts into those of the modern English-speaking world has a deeper purpose, however. The Bible demands that its readers come to its pages with the best preparation possible. We hope that this discussion of the ancient texts and the philosophies that often govern translations will prepare our readers to be more discerning and better-prepared readers of the Bible. Modern readers must still depend either on learning the ancient languages or on the skill of the translator(s). It may still be "Greek" to you, but we hope that this chapter has given you a better understanding of how that Greek (or Hebrew) text became the English text of the Bible you eventually choose.

And so we turn to the main task of this book: the analysis and evaluation of modern English translations of the Bible. Since they are the most familiar, and probably the most popular, our next chapter will focus on the verbal translations.

Suggested Readings

Greenlee, J. Harold. *Scribes, Scrolls, and Scripture: A Student's Guide to New Testament Textual Criticism*. Grand Rapids: William B. Eerdmans, 1985.

Metzger, Bruce M. *The Text of the New Testament: Its Transmission, Corruption, and Restoration*. New York: Oxford University Press, 1968.

CHAPTER 3

Verbal Translations

The pastor stood at the front door of the suburban church shortly after noon on a bright, sunny Sunday. Comfortable in the familiar surroundings, he greeted his parishioners as they filed out of the sanctuary and into the parking lot. The faces were as familiar as the greetings.

"Great sermon, Pastor," one intoned.

"Boy, you really stepped on our toes this morning," said another.

"Good service," still others offered, as they paused to shake his hand on their way out of the church.

"Thank you. Thank you for coming this morning. It was good to see you here," he replied.

Once in a while, someone's question on the way out the door would bring the receiving line to a halt. This time the question came from a man in his early thirties, a new member of the church, who, with his wife and two young children, was just becoming familiar with the congregation.

"I enjoyed your sermon, Pastor," he said, "but I noticed that what you read from the Bible didn't match what my Bible said. What translation are you using?"

"I was reading from the New International Version this morning," the pastor replied.

"Oh," said his wife. "Well . . . which Bible is the best translation? Should we buy a New International Version instead of the one we have?"

"The short answer to your question," said the pastor, aware that the line had stopped moving, "is that the translation you have is perfectly fine. But, if you don't already have plans, why don't you join us for dinner and we can talk about this further. I'd be happy to talk to you about the range of Bible translations and their strengths and weaknesses. Besides, this will give us a chance to get to know each other better."

"That sounds great, Pastor," they replied after a quick family conference.

Thirty years ago such a conversation in the vestibule might have filled any pastor with a sense of dread. In fact, depending on which parishioner raised the question, the pastor might have been facing a serious crisis in his or her ministry. Just a generation earlier, such a question would never have been asked; every member of the congregation would have been reading from the King James Version. Today, the variety of Bible translations present in any congregation on a given Sunday morning would astonish churchgoers of the 1940s and 1950s. We have grown accustomed to a variety of translations and expect our ministers or Sunday school teachers to read from a version that differs from our own.

The first two chapters of this book have traced the history of the canon's development, described some of the early translations of the Bible, and explored the wonders of textual criticism and translation philosophy. This chapter, and the next, sharpens our focus somewhat. We have been talking in general terms about the process and history of biblical translation; now we begin a conversation about the different translations themselves. As you will see, space does not allow us to address every available translation. We have chosen to discuss only the most popular and widely available versions. The focus of our discussion in this chapter is on "verbal" translations, or translations thatattempt to translate the Bible into modern English that is as close to the grammar, words, rhythm, and order of the ancient languages as possible. Our discussion includes a brief history, analysis, and evaluation of each translation.

King James Version

For over three hundred years, the King James Version (KJV) has been *the* Bible of the English-speaking church. Even though recent modern translations have gained in popularity at the expense of the KJV, it remains the standard of measure for all new translations. Students and church members often say—in all seriousness—that "if the King James Version was good enough for Jesus and Paul, it's good enough for me." Its impact on both worship and language is difficult to exaggerate. Long after we have abandoned the practice of our Puritan forebears, addressing one another as "thee" and "thou," people continue to use such language to address God. Even the words of Scripture that we have committed to memory are the words of the KJV.

To many people, the KJV *is* God's inspired word, and they will defend its honor to the bitter end. They will defend it in church, on the street corner, in the bookstore, in the newspaper, and on the Internet. Unfortunately many of these "defenders" are unaware of the history of the KJV, or of the changes that have been made to the version over the course of many years.

Toward the end of chapter 1 we summarized the events that led King James to convene a group of translators who produced a new translation, free from the marginal notes and comments that tended to offend one group within the English church or another. These leading biblical scholars of the day were to be guided by The Bishop's Bible and the original languages of Hebrew and Greek. Marginal notes would only be used to explain Hebrew and Greek words or to point out parallel passages. Distinctive type would set off any additional words that might be necessary to complete a thought, and chapter and verse divisions would remain the same. Dedicated to James I, the KJV was published in its entirety in 1611.

The great strength of this translation lies in the ability of the translators to capture the richness of the English language. Another strength stems from a similar ability on their part to use the vitality and energy of English poetry in the process of translation. Such attention to the poetic nature of language— especially to the way the translation would *sound* when read aloud—has much to do with the popularity and influence of the KJV.

In addition, the translators of the KJV must be given considerable credit for producing an excellent translation within their context. All translators work within the realities of the texts available, their knowledge of ancient languages, and the limits of modern language when used to express ancient ideas. The limitations of the KJV are those of history and language, rather than a reflection of the translators' skill and biblical understanding.

But, the KJV—as a modern English translation of the Bible—has significant limitations. Two strike at the heart of the translation, since they have to do with the languages in question: Hebrew, Greek, and English. A translation for some of the Hebrew words could only be

33

a conjecture in 1611, since the words in question were the only examples of those words available. With new discoveries of different Hebrew manuscripts—most notably the Dead Sea Scrolls—other examples became available, and the meanings of the words became much more clear. In the same way, more recent discoveries of ancient Greek manuscripts lend another dimension to the search for the meanings of such words. The translators of the KJV simply did not have such information available to them. A similar limitation of the translation is the result of changes in the English language over the past three hundred years. Some of the words commonly used in the 1600s are no longer in use today, and other words have taken on completely different meanings in that interval. As with any living language, words are added, taken away, or changed; in short, the modern English language is no longer that of King James's England.

An even more critical limitation, though, lies in the texts used by the KJV translators. In chapter 2 we mentioned textual criticism, the process by which one arrives at the text to be translated. In order to understand some of the criticism of the KJV, some further discussion of textual criticism may be helpful. Two basic theories of textual criticism are popular. The first assumes that the most correct reading is the one that appears in the most manuscripts; in other words, the *majority* rules. Doing textual criticism with this philosophy involves counting manuscript readings and determining a "winner." The other theory of textual criticism, more accepted among New Testament scholars, argues that each manuscript is descended from an earlier one (which it copied); eventually, every manuscript can be traced to an original (which, unfortunately, no longer exists). The descendants of each original are categorized by "families." Some families are thought to be older and more authentic than others; the manuscripts from these families carry more *weight* than others in making decisions about textual differences. Since most of the Greek manuscripts available today come from the Greek-speaking church, and can be dated after the Bible's translation into Latin by Jerome, these manuscripts and their readings may be outweighed by a manuscript that is part of an earlier family.

The discipline of textual criticism was a fledgling in the 1600s, and many of the earlier Greek manuscripts (belonging to earlier families) buried in the sands of Egypt were discovered long after the translators of the KJV were dead. Therefore, their translation was based on the readings they found in the majority of the manuscripts that were available to them. Unfortunately, in many places they were using a text that subsequent discoveries have proved to be incorrect and corrupt.

Such questions raise serious concerns about the KJV. These concerns are not serious enough to suggest that the KJV ought to be placed carefully on the shelf or in a museum and treated only as an artifact of a particular time and place in Christian history. They are serious enough, though, to suggest that the KJV ought not to be the only translation of the Scriptures used by Christians. Enough problems exist with this version to suggest the use of one or more modern translations as our primary translation(s). At the very least, such questions about the KJV open the door for more modern translations to challenge the dominance of the KJV in worship and Bible study.

The Revised Standard Version

In twentieth-century America, the *Revised Standard Version* (RSV) was the first such challenger. For almost one hundred years, church leaders and biblical scholars had sensed that changes in English usage were diminishing the effectiveness of the KJV. For this reason, the English church had commissioned a major revision (the Revised Version) of the KJV in the 1880s. An "Americanization" of that revision (incorporating the thoughts of American scholars on the revision committee) appeared in 1901, known as the American Standard Version. These revisions remained faithful to the text and language of the KJV. In fact, the publication and copyrighting of the ASV came as a response to what the preface to the RSV termed "unauthorized tampering" with the text of the RV in an attempt to introduce peculiarly American expressions into that text. The International Council of Religious Education, which held the copyright, formed a committee to study the need for further revisions. This committee recognized the changing nature of American English expressions and acknowledged recent discoveries of Greek manuscripts that had direct bearing on the text of the New Testament. It called for "a thorough revision of the version of 1901, which will stay as close to the Tyndale-King James tradition as it can in the light of our present knowledge of the Hebrew and Greek texts and their meaning on the one hand, and our present understanding of English on the other." A committee of thirty-two scholars, representing many

Protestant denominations in North America as well as twenty seminaries and colleges, began the translation in 1937. The New Testament was published in 1946. The entire Bible was published in 1951 and "authorized by a vote of the National Council of Churches of Christ in the U.S.A."

Perhaps the most noticeable difference between the KJV and the RSV is the modernization of the English language. Gone are many of the Elizabethan word endings; "sendeth" has become "sends," "goeth" has become "go," and "saith" has become "said." Also absent is the familiar "And it came to pass," often replaced by the more simple "After these things." Another change lies in the words used for direct address. Often "thee" and "thou" have been replaced by "you"; only when God is being addressed (or Jesus after the Resurrection) are the archaic forms retained.

Other changes involved stylistic considerations. Unlike earlier translations, the RSV printed poetic passages of the Old Testament in poetic form, rather than displaying them in paragraph form. Quotations marks were added, representing the translators' decisions about when discourse ends and narrative begins. (This is particularly difficult to establish in the Gospel of John, and some decisions by the translators [notably in John 3] have been criticized.) The translators decided to return to the practice of the KJV of using many different synonyms to translate one Hebrew or Greek word, reversing the practice of the RV and the ASV. Another reversal involved the decision to use "the LORD" in translating the divine name, as the RV and KJV had done, rather than substituting the incorrect construct, "Jehovah," of the ASV.

More striking to the careful reader, though, are the differences between the KJV and the RSV that come as a result of changes in the Hebrew and Greek texts themselves. Using the results of modern textual criticism, and taking advantage of recent manuscript discoveries, translators of both the original RSV and its revision in 1971 often chose to use a different text from that used by the translators of the KJV. Perhaps the most obvious changes were the omissions (in the original version) of the longer ending of Mark (16:9-20) and the story of the woman caught in adultery (John 7:53–8:11). These omissions caused significant furor, as evidenced by the fact that the most recent revisions of the RSV include such passages in the translation, along with marginal notes to remind the reader that such passages are not in the most ancient manuscripts.

The RSV received mixed reviews. Many approved of the new translation/revision, particularly in its attempt to use modern English without ignoring the literary quality found in the Tyndale-KJV tradition. Some thought the new translation far too conservative in modernizing the language, and they continued to produce their own translations. By far the most vocal critics, though, were those who considered the RSV to be almost sacrilegious in its attempt to supplant the KJV. Some attacked the theological bias of the RSV, most notably its tendency to translate passages in the Old Testament Prophets in a way that seemed to obscure their obvious reference to Jesus. A famous example is that of Isaiah 7:14; instead of "virgin" the RSV translated the Hebrew word as "young woman." Both are acceptable renderings of the same Hebrew word. The problem is that Matthew quotes Isaiah 7:14, using the Septuagint's Greek translation of the original Hebrew word. The Greek word may only be translated into English as "virgin." Critics of the RSV were sure that a theological bias against the virginal conception of Christ was at work here. They termed it the "Reviled Standard Version," they preached against its use from their pulpits, and some went so far as to burn it. They seized upon the fact that one of the members of the translation committee, though a noted expert on the Septuagint, was Jewish, and all manner of accusations were hurled at the committee itself.

Like the KJV, though, the RSV has quietly taken its place as one of the dominant English translations of the Bible. A number of commentaries were based on the RSV. Many churches and seminaries chose the RSV as their more-or-less "official" translation. More than likely, this is due to the conservative nature of the translation, as well as the broadly representative nature of the translation committee. In addition, unlike the KJV, the process of producing the RSV included provisions for ongoing revision, which allowed it to be revised as changes in usage occurred and as new textual discoveries (including that of the Dead Sea Scrolls) were made.

The RSV is readable and comfortable to many English-speaking Christians, Protestants and Catholics alike. For the most part its language will not offend anyone, even those who prefer the language of the KJV. The language is modern enough that it no longer sounds strange to ears used to late-twentieth-century English. The words and rhythms are not so different from that of the KJV, however, to be overly strange to ears accustomed to that older translation. The scholarly credentials of those involved in the initial translation project and those who have continued to oversee revisions in the RSV are impeccable. For this reason, the RSV became the version of choice for many seminaries. As young ministers graduated from those seminaries and went out into parish work, they took their RSVs with them into the churches. The RSV began to replace the KJV, particularly in those urban areas and among those denominations that had a large number of educated clergy.

The RSV has its weaknesses, though. The decision to return to the practice of the KJV of using a number of synonyms for the same Hebrew or Greek word may obscure meaning for the serious student of the Bible. Often biblical writers repeated a word for rhetorical effect. Such repetition was intentional on their part, designed to drive home the point of an argument or to alert the reader to a possible "play" on words. A similar problem results from the decision to modernize the words used for direct address. While we applaud such modern usage, modern English makes little provision for distinguishing between the plural and the singular "you." In fact, in many contexts, the reader has no way of knowing that the biblical text was addressed to "you" as a group of people rather than "you" as an individual. While this is not a huge difficulty, such confusion does play into the hands of the average American reader, who has a tendency to assume that "you" refers to her or him alone. Such a tendency toward individualism obscures the reality that biblical writers and readers rarely thought of themselves as individuals, and a great many of the biblical "you"s are plural. In all fairness, this problem is not exclusive to the RSV; every translation that does not distinguish in some way between the "you" singular and the "you" plural will fall victim to the same lack of clarity in interpretation.

In general, though, the RSV achieves its stated aims. Squarely in the tradition of the KJV, it is theologically and textually sound and accessible to the modern reader. The scholarship that stands behind it has made the RSV a fitting basis for many fine commentary and interpretation series.

The New American Standard Bible

The New American Standard Bible (NASB) is also in the tradition of the KJV, although it is only a cousin to the RSV. In 1901, a group of American scholars produced a revision of the KJV called the American Standard Version (ASV) designed to be the American equivalent of the British Authorized Version (AV). The ASV reflected the state of American biblical scholarship in the latter half of the nineteenth century; but, by the middle of the twentieth century, its language sounded stilted and archaic. Never as popular as either the KJV or the RSV, it has been exiled to the bookshelves of biblical scholars and libraries.

In its place the Lockman Foundation, a California not-for-profit corporation dedicated to Christian education, evangelism, and Bible translation, sponsored a new translation of the Bible. This translation was intended to carry on the legacy of the ASV, to translate the Scriptures with accuracy and fidelity to the original languages in both meaning and word order, while still producing a more "modern" translation. This translation was to be a *New* American Standard Bible, suitable for serious Bible study as well as public and private reading. It utilized the best Hebrew and Greek texts available and modernized the archaic language of the ASV. The NASB New Testament was published in stages from 1960 to 1963; the entire Bible followed in 1971.

The NASB is a conservative translation in almost every sense of the word. The NASB is unique among other versions in that it represents the most thorough attempt to produce a "verbal" equivalence translation of the ancient biblical texts. It often reproduces Hebrew and Greek tenses and meanings with fidelity, as well as following the ancient word order. The NASB is also conservative in its refusal to abandon traditional readings in the light of obvious textual evidence that supports a different reading. Examples of this conservative tendency may be found in the NASB's handling of Mark's ending (16:9-20/16:9) and the story of Jesus and the adulterous woman (John 7:53–8:11). In both cases, the textual problem is noted in the margin, and the text is set off by single brackets. The questionable passages are printed in the body of the text, devoid of almost any mark to distinguish them as problematic. In the case of Mark's ending, the NASB compounds the problem by printing (in italics) the so-called shorter ending of Mark (16:9) after 16:9-29, under the heading of "Addition." This presentation suggests that 16:9 is the only addition, rather than alerting the reader to the fact that both 16:9 and 16:9-20 are later additions to Mark's gospel, not found in any of the earlier Greek manuscripts.

By far the best testimony to its conservative nature, though, is the NASB's commitment to a "word-for-word" translation. As we mentioned above, this version is the most representative of the "verbal" equivalence philosophy of translation. Because of this, the translators produced a version that is particularly useful for serious Bible study. Its attention to word order and basic meaning makes it a great help to the person translating the Hebrew of the Old Testament or the Greek of the New Testament. Enterprising college and seminary students often use it for this very reason. With few exceptions, the NASB withstands close scholarly scrutiny, and its translation of those original texts is clear and faithful to the meaning of the original words.

But the greatest strength of the NASB is also its greatest weakness. In giving almost slavish attention to the word order and basic meaning of the ancient texts, this version offers a translation that is often wooden, stilted, and unsuitable for public reading. English is a language that pays particular attention to word order and structure; such word order often determines the sentence's meaning. Greek and Hebrew are quite different in this regard. The ancient languages can invert or rearrange word order for emphasis without changing the meaning of the sentence. Translating the ancient languages *in their word order* runs the risk of confusion at best, and it may distort the meaning of the passage. In addition, unlike its more "dynamic" cousins, the NASB may miss the meaning of an idiomatic expression in the ancient languages and translate the passage literally when a paraphrase might better have captured the meaning of the passage.

Another weakness lies in the format of the NASB. To be sure, the publishers should be given some credit for their innovative format. The biblical text is printed in a readable font. Marginal notes and cross-references to other biblical texts enhance the usefulness of this version. Each verse is indented from the left margin; however, this has the effect of obscuring the grammatical units (sentence, paragraph, etc.) that are so important to written English.

Even with its weaknesses, the NASB is a valuable resource for Bible study. Its ready accessibility and its fidelity to the ancient texts make this version very helpful to the person interested in serious study of the Bible.

The New American Standard Bible, Updated

In 1995, the Lockman Foundation published the NASB Update. As the name suggests, this was not a new version, but a revision, since almost twenty-five years had passed since the NASB had appeared. The process of updating the NASB included removing the words *thee* and *thou*, consulting the newest scholarly editions of ancient Hebrew, Aramaic, and Greek biblical texts, and removing some of the grammatical idiosyncracies found in the ancient languages that did not conform to English grammar. Some words were replaced with more modern equivalents, as well, and some sentences were rearranged in order to make them less confusing in English.

The NASB Update has addressed some of the criticisms leveled at its earlier sibling. While still committed to preserving the word order of the ancient texts, some concession has been made that word order is considerably more important to English than to Greek and Hebrew. This family of translations is also to be commended for its commitment to the best ancient texts scholarship can produce. The removal of obviously archaic language (e.g. *thee* and *thou*) should also make this update more palatable to modern ears. The cross-references and grammatical notes continue to be perhaps the best and most useful provided by any version.

Just as the NASB Update takes advantage of the strengths of the NASB, however, it must also continue to bear some of the criticisms. Fewer sentences begin with "and," but each verse continues to begin at the left margin. Unlike the NASB, the NASB Update has included section headings in a fashion similar to that employed by other versions. While helpful, these headings still do not allow the reader an immediate grasp of the syntactical structure of the passage. Also, like the NASB, the main strength of the NASB Update is still its main weakness: a translation that is intentionally as literal as possible.

On balance, the NASB Update is a step in the right direction. Those who have used the NASB will find the NASB Update to be just as useful. While still not very suitable for public reading, the NASB Update is certainly more fluid than the NASB, and it will sound less stilted. And the careful attention given to verb forms and translation in the NASB Update will continue to make this family of versions very useful for serious Bible study.

41

The New International Version

One of the more popular twentieth-century versions of the Bible is the NIV. By the time the entire NIV was published in 1978, it had advanced sales of more than one million copies. This new translation was motivated by a dissatisfaction with other existing translations within the "evangelical" Christian community, a dissatisfaction that seems to have been focused on the RSV. In the late 1950s and early 1960s a general discontent was expressed among conservative American Christians over certain problems with several translations, including the RSV. In 1965, responding to studies done by committees of the Christian Reformed Church and the National Association of Evangelicals, a group of scholars met to make plans for a new, more conservative, translation. This group formed a Committee on Bible Translation, made up of fifteen members, many of whom were biblical scholars and teachers. In 1967, their effort was significantly aided by an offer from the New York Bible Society (now the International Bible Society) to underwrite the translation project. Scholars from all over the English-speaking world came together over the next decade to accomplish this new translation.

The NIV was the product of teams and committees. Each book was assigned to a team of scholars. Their initial work in translation then went to an intermediate editorial committee which produced a revised translation. From there, a general editorial committee, thoroughly checked and revised the translation. Finally, this translation was edited and revised by the Committee on Bible Translation. In an attempt to ensure that the translation conformed to a readable and useful English style, the Committee on Bible Translation then submitted the entire Bible to a number of consultants for judgment on stylistic matters.

The result was a translation that has been widely accepted and praised for its scholarship *and* readability. Since all of those who participated in the project were publicly committed to the authority of the Bible as God's Word (each participant was required to indicate adherence to some written statement reflecting a high view of biblical authority) this version has acquired a reputation as *the* modern translation for the conservative/evangelical community. Part of the success of the NIV must also be attributed to the marketing efforts of Zondervan Press, which has been remarkably creative in its efforts to gain an ever-increasing market share for the translation. In particular, Zondervan has been one of the leaders over the past two decades in packaging this very successful translation with notes and commentary designed to appeal to a specific segment of the Bible-buying public.

The publication of the NIV did serve to increase the perception that major translations were now competing in the marketplace for the dollars of American Christians. Two "dynamic" versions, the Good News Bible and *The Living Bible*, had drawn significant attention away from the KJV versus RSV debate. The NIV offered what seemed to be a good compromise. It was an entirely new translation made by reputable scholars, many of whom were seminary and college teachers already known to a generation of ministers who had been their students. It also managed to capture a modern style without leaving the style and rhythm of the KJV too far behind. It was attractively published and bound and available in a number of different formats and bindings. Everyone interested in purchasing the NIV could find one in her or his price range. It lacked the obvious theological bias for which the RSV had so often been criticized. Churches placed the NIV in their pews, each volume attractively bound in a color to match the decor and stamped with the church's name in gold leaf. Large-print editions were available for those church members who could no longer read small print. In short, everything about the NIV was designed to ensure its success in a competitive market.

Despite some misgivings, we have chosen to discuss the NIV in the context of other "verbal" translations. The NIV is somewhat difficult to pin down at this point. It claims to be "eclectic" in its choice of ancient texts. Perhaps *eclectic* is a word that ought to be applied to its translation philosophy as well. At its heart, though, it is a "verbal" translation, seeking more often than not to remain true to the words and order of the ancient text. In many ways this results from the translators' attempt to produce a "conservative" translation. Such a philosophical position would make it difficult to include translation choices that seemed too "dynamic."

While the NIV claims to be based on an *eclectic* text, the preface to the NIV does not define *eclectic*. In textual criticism the word *eclectic* is usually reserved for that philosophy of textual criticism that neither counts manuscripts (the "majority" text underlying the KJV) nor holds too closely to the choice of the Alexandrian family of texts made by Wescott and Hort in their Greek text of the early twentieth century. The preface to the NIV noted clearly that the Old Testament was primarily based on the text published in the *Biblia Hebraica*, a standard scholarly text. Some information from other textual sources was used, but this Hebrew text provided a basis from which to work. No such reference to a scholarly edition was given for the New Testament, suggesting that the New Testament translators began by developing their own Greek text. All indications in the translation itself, though, suggest that the Greek text that underlies the NIV's New Testament is that of the United Bible Society (UBS, third edition). This also is a standard text for scholars around the world. One wonders why the translation committee didn't give credit to the edition.

The great strength of the NIV is its readability. It is probably the modern counterpart to the KJV in achieving a translation that is relatively easy to read and understand in public settings. At the same time, its language sounds familiar to people in church whose ears have been trained by the rhythms and sounds of the KJV. In short, it sounds "biblical" and "modern" at the same time. To be honest, this readability was accomplished through compromise. As we have already discovered in this chapter, those translations that are "verbal" must constantly balance the ancient and the modern languages in order to avoid sticking too closely to the ancient word order and syntax. As we shall see in the next chapter, those versions that are "dynamic" in nature have a similar concern, though their problem lies in becoming too interpretative and losing sight of the ancient texts altogether. The NIV committees attempted to walk this fine line, and, to their credit, usually achieved a good sense of balance between fidelity to the ancient texts and sensitivity to modern expression.

Another real strength of the NIV lies in its availability and usefulness in a number of different forms. Its format is attractive and inviting; the NIV was one of the first versions to make use of technological advances and marketing strategies to offer a product that almost everyone could use. It quickly became the standard translation, especially among those reading and studying the Bible in churches.

These strengths, however, also contribute to the weaknesses of the NIV. The primary weakness of this version results from the effort to achieve a readable translation. In order to be readable, the NIV often contains phrases that were too colloquial for a "verbal" translation. For instance, the powerful Old Testament formula "Thus says/saith Yahweh/the LORD" has become a rather insipid "This is what the Lord says" in the NIV. At other times, the same impulse toward readability and easy understanding results in translations that are far too interpretative in nature. One striking example is the NIV's tendency to translate the word *flesh* in the New Testament as "sinful nature," "human nature," and "human" (among others). Such ideas may be present in Paul's use of "flesh," but often Paul means to evoke the *range* of meanings that are part of the word *flesh*. The interpretative choices of the NIV translators, in this case, rob the text of its richness in an attempt to eliminate confusion.

Often, the "dynamic" nature of the NIV also causes another problem when using this version for serious Bible study. One of the characteristics of the modern English language (especially in the United States) is its tendency to avoid repeating the same word within a range of paragraphs or pages. We prefer to use synonyms to make the text more interesting and less repetitious. Ancient Hebrew and Greek, though, being primarily oral languages, used repetition in order to help the hearer or reader understand and remember the story or the argument. Repetition of words and phrases was also used for rhetorical effect. Recognizing such repetition is often an important part of interpreting biblical passages. Reading the passage in the NIV, though, may not allow the reader to recognize such textual characteristics, since the NIV has followed our modern preferences and used different words (synonyms) to translate the repeated word.

Two more weaknesses should be noted. Again, they are integrally related to what makes this a very strong and useful translation. We refer here to the stated philosophy of the translation project to produce a "conservative/evangelical" translation and the wedding of this philosophy with a marketing and advertising strategy. Careful comparison of this translation with other modern "verbal" translations suggests that, for the most part, the NIV is neither more nor less conservative than the others. What the NIV offers are conservative/traditional translations in those passages that have been the subject of considerable debate. For example, in Isaiah 7 the NIV preserves the translation "virgin" rather than "young woman." In other places in the Old Testament, though, the same Hebrew word that the NIV renders as "virgin" in Isaiah 7 is translated as "young woman." The conservative nature of the translation may also be seen in the notes that are provided. In the first place, a decision was made

45

to include as few notes as possible, in order to avoid confusing the reader. Many significant textual questions were ignored in the notes, giving the reader no indication of textual problems in the translation. Second, many of the notes that are provided reflect interpretative positions that match the conservative philosophy of the translators.

While certainly conservative in character, the NIV probably owes its conservative reputation more to the massive and pervasive advertising campaign waged on its behalf than to any noticeable characteristics of the version itself. Particularly unfortunate in this regard is the implication that all the other (competing) versions are somehow *not* conservative. Given the competitive nature of the Bible market, such a strategy raises serious questions about the "selling" of Scripture.

As a whole, the NIV receives higher marks than the previous discussion might suggest. Like any other modern translation of the Bible, the NIV should not be considered the *only* true translation. Its great achievement, though, lies in its readability. No other modern English translation has reached the same level and still maintained such a close connection to the ancient languages.

The New International Reader's Version

The *The New International Reader's Version* (NirV) is designed to make the Bible accessible to the large number of people in the United States with limited literacy in English. It is not an entirely new translation, but it has been based on the text of the NIV. Sentences have been shortened and simplified, and difficult or long words have been modified. This version is aimed at children below the age of eight, adults who read at or below the fourth-grade level, and the growing number of people in the United States for whom English is a second language. In addition, it contains a dictionary and numerous other helps designed to ease the inexperienced reader into the process of reading the Bible.

In essence, the NirV is another attempt to meet the demand for Bibles that are easily accessible. In fact, it is being advertised as a beginning step. One is introduced to the Bible through the NirV, then one steps up to the NIV. Also, as is evidenced by the explosion of different formats already taking advantage of this simplified version, the marketing possibilities are endless.

This is not a version for study or public worship. This is a version with "training wheels." While it may be very useful for the "target" audience, the NirV ought not to be used except when faced by a specific situation of limited literacy. It is certainly accessible to almost anyone, but it is a temporary solution at best.

The New American Bible

We noted in an earlier chapter that, in addition to those translations of the Bible aimed at the Protestants of the English-speaking world, there were also translations for English-speaking Catholics. The first of these was the Douay-Rheims version, translated by and for English Catholics exiled to France during the late 1500s and early 1600s. It was soon revised by Bishop Challoner (1750). Since the Roman Catholic Church recognized only Jerome's Vulgate as canonical Scripture, these earliest English translations intended for Catholic audiences and worship were translations from the Latin of the Vulgate, rather than the ancient Hebrew and Greek.

In 1943, Pope Pius XII changed the face of Catholic biblical scholarship and translation. His encyclical on Scripture studies, *Divino afflante Spiritu*, encouraged Catholic biblical scholars to turn their attention to the ancient biblical languages. In response to that papal encouragement, American Catholic bishops also called for a new translation of the ancient texts into an English Bible that would be suitable both for individual study and for worship. This call produced the New American Bible (NAB). An Old Testament was ready by 1969, and the entire Bible was published in 1970. The NAB New Testament was a successor to the Confraternity Version, a project that had been in the works for some decades among American Catholic scholars. The entire process took on a sense of urgency when the use of English (the "vernacular") in worship began in 1964.

The translators working on this original edition of the NAB followed a translation philosophy of "dynamic equivalence." The reason for its inclusion here is the revision of the NAB-NT, published in 1986 to replace the 1970 New Testament. In that revision, the translation philosophy changed from "dynamic" to "verbal." A similar revision is in progress for the NAB-OT.

Like most of the translations produced in the last fifty years, the NAB made use of standard critical texts of the Old and New Testaments. Where the translation team felt it necessary, other textual evidence for the Old Testament was used instead of the Masoretic Hebrew Text. More often than not, the Nestle-Aland/UBS text of the New Testament was the basis for both the original and the revised NAB-NT. Some scholars have disagreed with the committee's choice of texts in certain OT passages, but most of the NAB-OT has been translated from texts that are acceptable in scholarly circles.

Since this translation is specifically aimed at the American Catholic community, it has left the NAB open to suspicions of theological bias. Although evidence of such bias does not discredit the NAB as a very good modern translation, enough readings (and notes) are present to mark the theological tendencies of this version. As expected, the woman in Isaiah 7 is, without question, a "virgin," and a note reminds us of the implications of such an interpretation. References to "brothers" of Jesus remain in the New Testament, but footnotes inform us that the Greek word used in the ancient world often referred to any kind of relative, not necessarily to siblings with the same parents. In all fairness, though, one note (on Mark 6:3) also indicates that it is only the Catholic church's doctrine of the perpetual virginity of Mary that raises any interpretative doubts about the nature of Jesus' siblings at all. Such theological notes are fewer and more balanced than one might expect, given the fact that the NAB would need official approval from the church in order to be used in worship.

The NAB is the product of a thoughtful and careful translation process. The revision of the NAB-NT is a step in the right direction, especially in meeting the need for a study Bible that places the best of modern critical scholarship in the hands of educated and devout church members. Although it does not make a strong claim to be an ecumenical translation, the NAB translation committee did include some Protestant members. For this reason, the NAB is useful not only for devout American Catholics, but also for those Protestants who desire more understanding of Catholic biblical scholarship.

Interestingly, the criticism of the NAB has not come from Protestant scholars and reviewers, but rather from those Catholics who object to the gender-inclusive language of the translation. Admittedly, this is a question that must be dealt with as a matter of philosophy, particularly when one desires to produce a "verbal equivalency" translation. The forms of the ancient languages rarely leave doubt as to the gender of the word in question, but some words have a different gender reference in English from that possessed in the ancient languages. The process of translation always involves interpretation and paraphrase, even in those translations that attempt to maintain as close a connection as possible to the ancient languages. It is not our purpose here to settle (or even argue) the question of gender-inclusive language. What we will say in reference to the NAB, however, is that it represents a very genuine (but cautious) attempt to be gender inclusive in its language, and it certainly does not deserve most of the criticism directed against it.

The NAB is a welcome addition to the competitive world of late-twentieth-century translations of the Bible. Like other translations, it suffers from the problems that arise from the process of trying to translate the words and meanings of ancient texts into the modern English language—without losing something on either side of the process. For the most part, though, the NAB succeeds in providing a readable, scholarly, and usable translation, filling a much-needed denominational niche. One must also applaud the decision to revise both the NAB-NT and the NAB-OT. Such a revision process can only enhance the NAB's stature among other translations.

The New King James Version

The economic success of the NIV seems to have inspired the publication of The New King James Version (NKJV). On the one hand, the success of the NIV showed that a considerable market existed for new, more modern translations aimed at conservative American Christians. On the other hand, conservative translation or not, many of the new versions were being criticized for challenging the dominance of the KJV. In 1982/1983, Thomas Nelson Publishers of Nashville, Tennessee, introduced The New King James Version of the Bible. It was a new translation from the Hebrew and Greek texts, although it followed the same textual principles as its revered parent, the KJV. Most of all, this translation was designed to recapture that part of the Bible market consisting of persons who were no longer comfortable with the language of the seventeenth century, but who really didn't want to give up reading the KJV.

Enter the NKJV. Here was a translation that claimed to maintain the order, power, and grace of the version that, in the English-speaking world, had become synonymous with the Bible. Here was a version that also claimed to offer the same fidelity to the ancient texts and the same attention to public readability. Here was a version that would modernize the language of the translation, but still retain the familiar phrasing and rhythm of the KJV. It would be new, but not *too* new.

The philosophy of translation expressed in the preface, and embodied in the version itself, leaves no doubt as to the purpose of this new translation. Most important, the translators of the NKJV were guided by their reverence for the KJV itself. Their statements that the translators (in 1611) were "almost as familiar with the original languages of the Bible as with their native English" and that "their reverence for the divine Author and His Word assured a translation of the Scriptures in which only a principle of utmost accuracy could be accepted" certainly suggest that no subsequent version had attained the high standard of the KJV. The translators of *those* versions could match neither the linguistic facility nor the piety of the translators of the KJV. Beyond that, the NKJV makes it clear that the majority text, on which foundation the KJV had been laid (for lack of any better textual information at the time), is a far more stable basis for an accurate modern translation. The editors and translators of the NKJV are aware of other text-critical philosophies that challenge the majority text; they merely prefer the majority or "received" text.

The NKJV is open to one of the most devastating criticisms leveled at the KJV, without being able to point to limitations of history and language. The KJV translators had little choice but to use the majority or "received" text in 1611; most of the earlier manuscripts lay as yet undiscovered. Given their academic excellence and deep reverence for the Bible, one would suppose that they would use the best text available, no matter what difficulties it posed. Any "reverence" for the text in the NKJV, however, seems to be for the English text of the KJV, rather than for the ancient texts of the Bible.

The translation itself does little more than update the language of the KJV. Archaic forms ("thee" and "thou," "sayeth" and "sayest") have been eliminated in favor of more modern speech patterns. Places where the KJV is known to be inaccurate in its grammar and idiom have been corrected and smoothed over. Throughout, the language conforms to more modern usage. Even in this, however, the NKJV has been criticized for producing a text with language that was never really used by any generation of English-speaking people.

It is a curious combination of the new and the old: a new patch on an old garment.

The NKJV has never really succeeded in supplanting either the KJV itself or taking much away from the other modern English translations. In fact, a recent *USA Today* article showed the NKJV with a modest percentage of sales (about 10 percent). Its publication raises more questions about translations, translation philosophy, and one's allegiance to a particular translation than it answers.

The 21st Century King James Version

While the KJ21 is unlikely to be as widely known as the NKJV, it warrants our attention at this point. The KJ21 is the project of William Prindele, a retired attorney. Convinced that the scholarship and literary artistry of the translators who produced the 1611 KJV remains unmatched today, Mr. Prindele formed a publishing company whose primary purpose was to produce, market, and distribute a modern version of that 1611 masterpiece. The KJ21, published in 1994, is the culmination of a process that used *Webster's New International Dictionary, Second Edition, Unabridged,* as the authority on the modern English language through which to modernize the wording of the 1611 KJV. If Webster considered a word to be archaic or offered a more clear and modern synonym, the word was changed. In this way none of the majesty and artistry of the translation was lost, but the translation became significantly more clear to the modern reader.

Without apology or pretense, Prindele and his publishing company have chosen to build their Bible on the foundation of the KJV. As we have noted above, such a foundation includes a text that contains a considerable number of questionable readings. Any weaknesses resulting from using the majority text will also affect this version. Prindele is aware of the textual controversy, and he has chosen to accept the consequences of basing his translation on such a foundation. To him, the benefits of remaining firmly in the KJV tradition far outweigh the problems. A second weakness results from an attempt to distinguish between certain types of biblical texts by using different typefaces. While this may seem, at first, to be a helpful tool for the reader, such a practice graphically highlights some of the text as more important than other portions. In fact, those passages that are "less familiar, less frequently quoted and memorized, and less frequently included in lectionaries and for sermon texts, but

51

which are of specific interest to Bible scholars, historians, and social scientists" are printed in the smallest readable type possible. This message is clear: these passages are not really as important as the rest of the Bible. Finally, the KJ21 seems to have fallen into the trap of advertising exaggeration. It consistently claims to be rescuing the Bible (the KJV) from the ravages of modern translations, most of which are the products of "modern liberal" scholars.

On a positive note, however, Prindele's version does have the advantage of being honest about the modernization process. One can applaud his honesty and diligence, even if one disagrees with his starting point.

Finally, Prindele is now in the process of working on what will be entitled *The Third Millennium Bible* (TMB). For many years now, the KJV has not included the Apocrypha. Prindele's company is at work on a modernized version of the Apocrypha, which was included in the 1611 translation, and the TMB will include not only a modernized KJV (the KJ21), but a modernized Apocrypha as well.

The New Jerusalem Bible

That we have chosen to discuss this version in the chapter devoted to "verbal" translations is another reminder that the dividing line between "verbal" and "dynamic" remains somewhat fluid. While the Jerusalem Bible (JB, published in 1966 and revised in 1973) will be considered in the next chapter on "dynamic" translations and "paraphrases," its revision, the New Jerusalem Bible (NJB), moved to the "verbal" side of that line. Some have argued that it did not move far enough in that direction.

The NJB was published in 1986, and a Reader's Edition followed in 1989. Like the NAB and the JB, this Reader's version is designed to be used both for worship and for study. The JB and NJB, though, are intended more to be study Bibles than liturgical tools. For that reason, they include well-written introductions to sections of the Bible, helpful introductions to each book, and explanatory notes. The JB was primarily a translation into English of *La Bible de Jerusalem*, a French translation that was the product of a French Catholic university in Jerusalem, L'Ecole Biblique. While critics have often challenged the translations produced in this family, they have also praised the quality of scholarship found in the notes and introductions. In addition, the JB was one of the first *modern* versions to use a format that printed the Bible to resemble other books.

The JB used both the ancient textual traditions and the French translation, producing a translation that often followed the French tradition more accurately than it followed the ancient languages. Therefore, the NJB made a point of translating directly from the ancient texts, using the French tradition only when the words of the ancient manuscripts were not clear. In addition, the JB followed a "dynamic" (almost paraphrastic) philosophy of translation, striving to produce a version with literary and stylistic flair. While such a philosophy (and the aid of literary geniuses such as J. R. R. Tolkien) sometimes resulted in magnificent and insightful translations, the JB was often criticized for interpreting the biblical text rather than translating it. Such criticism over the space of some twenty years prompted a wholesale revision; thus we have the NJB.

This version remains a study Bible rather than a translation primarily intended for worship or private devotional use. While a reader's edition of the NJB has also been published, it is clearly dependent on the original format. The preface to the Reader's Edition makes it clear that some questions will be raised that can only be answered by consulting the full-study NJB. As a study Bible, the overwhelming strength of the NJB remains its introductory and explanatory material. This material is the product of some of the finest Catholic biblical scholarship. It is balanced in its approach, and it takes full advantage of the scholarly work on the Bible done in the last two centuries. Like the NAB, the NJB is designed for a Catholic audience. It contains the entire range of books considered canonical by the Catholic communion, including those of the Apocrypha, and has printed them in canonical order. Protestant readers should not be surprised if notes and introductory material sometimes support Catholic doctrinal positions on passages that have been disputed since the Reformation.

More surprising are the times that the NJB does not support such doctrine. For instance, in Isaiah 7:14 (one sure test passage), the NJB translates the Hebrew as "young woman," rather than following the Greek (LXX) translation of "virgin." The NJB does, however, provide an excellent note explaining the choice of the LXX and the resulting Jewish tradition, which Matthew sees as a prophecy of the virginal conception of Jesus. Unlike the NAB, the NJB does not tread carefully around references in the Gospels to "brothers" and "sisters" of Jesus.

A note to Matthew 12:46 points out that the Greek word translated as "brother" may also mean "close relative," but neither the translations nor the notes lay out or defend the doctrine of the perpetual virginity of Mary.

The weaknesses of the NJB are quite similar to those of the NIV. While less "dynamic" than its predecessor (the JB), the NJB still tends to consider fidelity to the modern expression of English more important than accuracy in translating the ancient manuscripts. To be sure, this revision ought to help the reader follow theological arguments, which depend on the author's word choice and wordplay. Such improvements, though, draw attention to the NJB's tendency to interpret rather than translate. A more literal translation of Paul's Greek may not permit a smoothly flowing, readily understandable English passage. The NJB, like the NIV, tends to rearrange Paul's language and clarify it, at once changing and narrowing Paul's meaning. Such changes are subtle; perhaps our criticism is too stringent. Such changes do, however, characterize those translations that tend toward the "dynamic," and a reader ought to be aware of the character of any chosen translation.

One final note on the NJB. Like many other modern English translations, the NJB has made a conscious attempt to be inclusive in its language. It is perhaps the most conservative translation in this regard, since it does not address the question of gender-inclusive references to God or find a new word with which to translate the Greek *adelphos* (brother). The translators of the NJB were aware of the need to pay careful attention to the built-in gender bias of both the ancient and modern languages, though, and add another voice to the growing call for sensitivity and thoughtfulness in translating such an important book as the Bible.

The NJB has retained more of the rhythm and structure of the ancient languages than the JB, particularly in the Old Testament. This characteristic, combined with a continued attention to the literary and stylistic flow of the translation, will make the NJB more suitable for public reading and worship than was the JB. The NJB continues to provide an attractive option for Roman Catholic readers, who may now choose either the NAB, the NJB, or the NRSV. The reader will often find this version to be refreshingly different; but, in light of its interpretative tendencies, it probably ought to be read alongside other translations.

The New Revised Standard Version

As its name suggests, The New Revised Standard Version (NRSV) is part of the family of translations that began with Tyndale and the KJV. Like many of the other "verbal" translations discussed in this chapter, the NRSV was guided by two main principles: fidelity to the ancient biblical languages and reverence for the literary and formal tradition begun by the KJV. In addition to these principles, the editor's comments to the reader in the NRSV noted other concerns that resulted in a new translation. The first of these was a series of scholarly and textual discoveries that had an impact on the texts underlying the Old Testament of the RSV. Changes in that text made a revision necessary. The second concern was related to the language and culture of English-speaking America. On the one hand, expressions and idioms of the language continued to change; some phrases used in the 1950s no longer had the same meaning twenty years later. On the other hand, many in the church had raised questions about the exclusiveness of the Bible's language, particularly in passages where the ancient languages themselves used words that were inclusive in nature. These concerns, philosophical as well as cultural, prompted the Policies Committee of the Revised Standard Version (a part of the National Council of Churches) to approve a thorough revision of the RSV. After some fifteen years (1974–89), the NRSV was published.

Like its predecessor, the NRSV is a translation based on the most accepted scholarly versions of the ancient texts. In fact, since some members of the translation committee of the NRSV were also members of the committee working on a new edition of the Greek New Testament, the NRSV committee members had access to any changes to be made in that new edition. Like the RSV, the NRSV translators were concerned with producing a version that would be suitable for serious Bible study as well as one that would be readable and useful for public worship. Within those constraints, though, the primary purpose for producing the new translation was to update and clarify the language of the RSV. A more modern translation was necessary.

For the most part, scholars (who were already disposed to accept the RSV as a useful successor to the KJV) have considered the NRSV to be a success. Even the editorial preface to the NRSV admits that "no translation of the Bible is perfect or is acceptable to all groups of readers," and most reviewers have discovered passages that they might have changed. The overall evaluation of the NRSV, though, has been a positive one. As one of the latest entries into the marketplace, the NRSV was able to use the results of the tremendous amount of scholarly attention that has been given to the study of the Bible in recent decades. As one of the newer translations, the NRSV was also able to take advantage of changes in the modern English language. In this regard, translations such as the NRSV continue to seek a balance between fidelity to the ancient texts and readability in a modern context. With few exceptions, the NRSV has managed to achieve this balance as well as any "verbal" translation.

This is perhaps the greatest strength of the NRSV: it achieves a more modern translation that is somewhat similar to the language of the KJV yet is acceptable to modern readers. It is also particularly *American* English. Another vote for the NRSV has come from many of the scholarly "study" or "annotated" editions. Not long after the publication of the NRSV itself, this translation was used by publishers such as Oxford, Cambridge, and HarperCollins as the basis of their study editions. This merely adds to the strength of an already useful translation.

Careful attention to modern forms of language has resulted in changes designed to update the language of the RSV. For example, Psalm 50:9 has been changed from "I will take no bull from your house" (RSV) to "I will not take a bull from your house" (NRSV). And Paul's statement in 2 Corinthians 11:25 has been modified to read "I received a stoning" (NRSV) instead of "I was stoned" (RSV). Obviously, the way Americans use the English language has changed since the early 1950s. This change is nowhere more evident than in the use of (and argument for using) gender-inclusive language. As we have noted above, considerable attention has been paid in our society to the use of exclusive language, particularly since it reflects an often subconscious bias. For this reason, the NRSV committee was charged with eliminating exclusive language when such elimination did not destroy the meaning of the ancient languages. Some words in those ancient texts were intended to be gender inclusive, but the languages had few, if any, words that would make such intentions clear. Therefore, the language was nominally masculine; such words could easily be translated with more inclusive terms, and they would then reflect more clearly the intention of the text itself.

For their efforts to accomplish this purpose, the translation committee of the NRSV has been rather severely criticized by both sides. Some have argued that the NRSV goes too far with inclusive language and transgresses the meaning of the text. Others have argued that it did not go nearly far enough; inclusive language is used inconsistently and could have been employed more often. In particular, these critics have disagreed with the restrictions placed on the use of inclusive language by the various committees in charge of the translation. The translation committee was given the mandate to use inclusive language wherever possible when referring to human beings. These critics would like to have seen such language extended to references to God as well. To be fair, many of these critics (on both sides) have begun their analyses by welcoming the fact that an attempt was made to be more inclusive in language.

As is so often the case, what is seen as a strength of the translation may also be a significant weakness. So it is with this question of inclusive language in the NRSV. And the discussion which followed resulted in the publication of the NRSV in a significantly different format.

The New Testament and Psalms: An Inclusive Version

In 1995, Oxford Press unveiled a new version of the NRSV, one that had been edited in order to

> *replace or rephrase all gender-specific language not referring to particular historical individuals, all pejorative references to race, color, or religion, and all identifications of persons by their physical disability alone, by means of paraphrase, alternative renderings, and other acceptable means of conforming the language of the work to an inclusive idea.* (pp. viii-ix; italics in the original)

Immediately dubbed the "PC" (Politically Correct) Bible, this inclusive version became the focus of reports on CNN and in the *Wall Street Journal*. It generated considerable publicity, which probably aided sales of the volume. More important, though, the publicity brought the question of inclusive language back into the public eye.

This new version of the NRSV is unlikely to challenge the popularity of other "verbal" translations. Its attempt to address the issue of inclusive language for God will make it an item of interest for libraries and scholars but of questionable value for others. Its language is just too strikingly different to be acceptable to the broad range of Bible readers. Anyone who has tried to use gender-inclusive language in a consistent manner will be aware of how difficult, and often cumbersome, such a process becomes. The root of the problem is that most languages (English among them) use pronouns that possess gender. To be consistently inclusive, one must either avoid pronouns or add references to the other gender. Both strategies are quite awkward. While the idea of God as "Father-Mother" may be theologically sound, the phrase will not gain ready acceptance among most churchgoers in the immediate future.

This version goes beyond the debate over gender-inclusive language to address other barriers to full inclusion in the church. Citing Luther's translation of the Bible into German as an example of the Bible's power over language, the editors of this volume tried "to *anticipate* developments in the English language with regard to specificity about a number of issues such as gender, race, and physical disability" (p. viii; italics in the original). Therefore, this version will refer to "enslaved people," "people with leprosy," and "blind people." Even references to God's "right" hand will be translated in terms of power or nearness, rather than "right" or "left," presumably so as not to exclude those who might be "left-handed persons."

It is certainly not our intention to dismiss this version or treat it flippantly. Its very presence bears testimony to the sensitivity with which Christians are beginning to treat one another and those outside the church. One can certainly also make a strong case for understanding the ministry of Jesus as one of including the excluded. But this version's attempt to influence the modern English language, rather than to translate the ancient texts faithfully, crosses the line from translation into interpretation. It presents the Bible as it *should be*, not as it is.

This "inclusive" version will certainly fill an important niche in the landscape of modern English translations of the Bible. Perhaps it will influence some translators to change their use of language. It may influence popular perceptions of gender identity as it relates to God. But it is unlikely to have a major impact on the process or progress of translating the Bible.

As for the NRSV itself, one suspects that the number of people who choose to use this version will continue to grow slowly. Given the large number of new translations that have appeared in recent years, it seems difficult to imagine that any new translation will be able to have the immediate impact of the NIV, or even the RSV. As the basis of important study editions, though, the NRSV may be used more widely. It also combines ease of readability in public with scholarly clarity for Bible study. This combination should ensure its increasing popularity.

Conclusion

One can see why the pastor didn't take the time to give his church members the "long" answer. The answer to the question, "Which translation should I use?" is rather lengthy. And this chapter is merely the beginning. We have looked at those translations that are "verbal" in nature. Along the way, we have noted that the KJV continues to be a popular translation among those Christians who speak English. We have also noted that the last half-century has seen an ever-increasing number of new translations, each one of which claims to be the most accurate, the most innovative, the most conservative, the most liberal, the most readable, or the most something else.

For all of the attention to theological and philosophical differences in translating the Bible, the commercialization of the Bible publishing industry is difficult to ignore. Many new versions, no matter how much they claim to be answering a theological need, seem most designed to meet the demand in American culture for something that is "new and improved." Even the Bible has fallen victim to the demands of consumerism.

The reader who is looking for a Bible that will be understandable, useful for study, and easily read in public must somehow sort out all of these conflicting claims and choose a Bible. This chapter has offered only half an answer to the question. The "dynamic" translations and "paraphrases" await.

Suggested Readings

Bailey, Lloyd R., ed. *The Word of God: A Guide to English Versions of the Bible*. Atlanta: John Knox, 1982.

Kubo, Sakae, and Walter Specht. *So Many Versions? Twentieth-Century English Versions of the Bible*. Grand Rapids: Zondervan, 1975.

Lewis, Jack P. *The English Bible from KJV to NIV: A History and Evaluation*. Grand Rapids: Baker Book House, 1981.

CHAPTER 4

Dynamic Translations and Paraphrases

A voice from the back of the classroom interrupted Dr. Jones's lecture on the Lord's Prayer.

"Dr. Jones, I have a question."

Turning from the blackboard, Dr. Jones directed her attention toward the speaker, a young student in his early twenties.

"Go ahead, Bill," she said.

"We've been talking about the Lord's Prayer here in Matthew 6, and I notice that my Bible translates the last part of the prayer much differently than the way you just read it."

"What version are you using, Bill? And what does it say?" asked Dr. Jones.

"Well, my mother gave me a new Bible for my birthday. It's called *The Message*. It doesn't include verse numbers at all, and it translates the very end of the prayer in an interesting way. Let me read it:

"'Keep us safe from ourselves and the devil. You're in charge! You can do anything you want! You're ablaze in beauty! Yes. Yes. Yes.'

"Now, Dr. Jones, to me that sounds nothing like the prayer that you just read. Your version was much closer to the way I learned the prayer. How can two Bibles be so different?"

Dr. Jones looked back at her NRSV Bible. "Bill, let me point out two things about the differences between The New Revised Standard Version and *The Message*. First, the NRSV is a verbal translation that attempts a word-for-word translation of the Greek. *The Message* is a paraphrase and not a translation. Its purpose is to transform the language of more formal English translations into the kind of English you might speak with a close friend.

"Second, remember that between these two versions is a third kind of translation known as a dynamic-equivalence translation, which attempts to elicit from us today the same kind of response that the earliest readers of the Bible made to the text. These translations attempt a phrase-by-phrase translation so that the Bible reads as if it were written in English and not translated from another language."

Bill shook his head in confusion. "Can you tell us which versions of the Bible belong in the category of dynamic translations and paraphrases?" he asked.

Like Bill, many people today are confused about the differences between verbal, dynamic, and paraphrased versions of the Bible. We have already explained these differences in chapter 2. And, in chapter 3, we explored the history of verbal translations and analyzed the major English versions of the Bible that fit into this category. Now we turn our attention to the increasingly popular dynamic and paraphrased versions that are widely available in English.

Dynamic Translations

For over one hundred years, Bible translators have attempted to translate the Bible from the ancient languages of Hebrew, Greek, and Aramaic in order to offer a readable Bible in common, everyday English. These dynamic versions differ from verbal translations in that their primary purpose is to capture the flavor of the ancient language in modern English and not to worry much at all about a word-for-word translation.

The dynamic-equivalence theory was first proposed by Eugene Nida as an approach to biblical translation that might assist Bible translators in various cultural contexts. Cecil Hargreaves has identified two mainstream movements in English Bible translation that emerged during the twentieth century and which, for the most part, were restricted to dynamic translations. The first movement, called a general idiomatic approach, was launched by translators like James Moffatt, Edgar Goodspeed, J. B. Phillips, and Ronald Knox, who viewed their translations as phrase-for-phrase efforts to reproduce the meaning of the text in modern English. In the words of Phillips, their goal was to make the translation "not sound like a translation at all." This task was accomplished by modernizing phrases in the Bible that are often misunderstood by English speakers today.

A second movement among dynamic translations, known as the common language approach, emerged later as a result of efforts by the American Bible Society to use linguistic analysis to translate Bibles in international mission contexts. This movement spawned such translations as Today's English Version (later known as the *Good News Bible*) and The Contemporary English Version. Extensive linguistic analysis and theories about the communication of meaning from one language to another provided the theoretical foundation for these common language translations.

Dynamic translations are often easily identified either by subtitles that draw attention in some form or fashion to the modern language nature of the version or by catchy titles that generate a popular appeal. Recent dynamic translations of the general idiomatic variety include J. B. Phillips's The New Testament in Modern English (1958), the Jerusalem Bible (1966), the New English Bible (1970) along with the Revised English Bible (1989), the New Century Bible (1991), and the *New Living Translation* (1996). This last version is a revision of *The Living Bible*, a popular paraphrase, which will be discussed later in this chapter.

Common language translations include the Good News Bible: Today's English Version (NT, 1966; entire Bible, 1976) and the Contemporary English Version (NT, 1991; entire Bible, 1995), both published by the American Bible Society.

Early Twentieth-Century Dynamic Translations

A number of dynamic translations were produced in the first half of the twentieth century. The Twentieth Century New Testament, published in 1901–2, was the first widely accepted English translation of the modern era. About 1890, two British laypersons named Mary K. Higgs and Ernest Malan approached W. T. Stead, editor of the *Review of Reviews*, with their concern that children could not understand the English of the King James Version. At Stead's insistence, Higgs and Malan cooperated in translations of the Gospels and Acts. Later they were joined by thirty-five other people, half of whom were ministers and half laypersons.

This translation provided a means for native-English speakers to "read the most important part of their Bible in that form of their own language which they themselves use." The preface noted that "the

English of the Authorized Version (King James) . . . is in many passages difficult, or even quite unintelligible to the modern reader."

Interestingly, the translators elected to print the Bible with the books of the New Testament arranged in chronological order. A reprint by Moody Press in 1961 restored the books to their canonical order and updated Britishisms, such as the use of pounds in the Parable of the Talents and references to "the gaol." This version was frequently consulted by the translation committee of Today's English Version some sixty years after its initial publication, a testimony to its reputation among biblical scholars.

One of the scholars who served as a consultant to The Twentieth-Century New Testament was Richard Francis Weymouth, a fellow at University College in London and a classical scholar. His own translation appeared in 1903, the year after his death, and was entitled The New Testament in Modern Speech, An Idiomatic Translation into Everyday English. Several editions of his work have been published, with a considerable revision appearing in 1924.

Weymouth's translation is interesting for at least two reasons. First, he uses his own Greek text for the translation, entitled The Resultant Greek New Testament. And second, he indicates that his purpose is not "to supplant the Versions already in general use" but rather to "furnish a succinct running commentary to be used side by side with its elder compeers." To this end, he translated the New Testament into "the English of the present day" in a way that "the inspired writer himself would have expressed his thoughts, had he been writing in our age and country."

In 1924, Helen Montgomery published a highly respected translation of the New Testament entitled The Centenary Translation. This translation commemorated the one hundredth anniversary of the American Baptist Publication Society. Montgomery's purpose was to "make a translation chiefly designed for the ordinary reader, intended to remove the veil that a literary or formal translation inevitably puts between the reader of only average education and the meaning of the text."

Montgomery, a native of New York and an 1880 graduate of Wellesley College, worked with several agencies of the Northern Baptist Convention and, in 1921, was elected the first female president of that denomination. A good friend of Susan B. Anthony and Frances Willard, Montgomery was a strong supporter of women's suffrage and worked aggressively to open the University of Rochester to women students.

Montgomery's translation is noteworthy for its chapter and paragraph headings, which provide immediate orientation to the subject of a passage. Interesting paragraph headings include "Prayer's *Magna Charta*" in Matthew 7, "Jesus' Challenge to Race Prejudice" in Luke 4, and "Hogs Mean More than Men" in Luke 8. She also took considerable pains to set quotations apart from the text by means of italics and indentations. The small size of the volume and low price were intended "to stimulate the daily reading of the Gospels."

Several other early translations of and commentaries on the Bible were undertaken by women. Julia E. Smith Parker, an American, produced a translation in 1876 that is best described as a verbal translation. Some scholars have called it a "pony" of the original text because Parker's philosophy was to ignore context, translating each Greek and Hebrew word with the same English word or phrase each time it occurred.

Also, Elizabeth Cady Stanton prepared a commentary on those portions of the Bible related to women, which was published in 1895 as *The Woman's Bible*. Its purpose was "to revise only those texts and chapters referring to women, and those also in which women are made prominent by exclusion." A reviewing committee assisted Stanton in preparing the commentary and translation of selected texts.

James Moffatt, a Scottish pastor and biblical scholar and arguably the best-known Bible translator in the first half of the twentieth century, published *A New Translation of the Bible* in 1928. This volume combined two previous and quite popular translations of the two testaments, *The New Testament: A New Translation* which appeared in 1913 and *The Old Testament: A New Translation*, published in 1924. Moffatt's stellar teaching career included stints at Mansfield College at Oxford University, the United Free Church College in Glasgow, Scotland, and Union Theological Seminary in New York City.

The popularity of Moffatt's translation set the standard by which later dynamic versions of the Bible would be judged. It was based upon Hermann von Soden's 1913 edition of the Greek text with which many textual critics have taken issue. Moffatt's purpose was "to convey to the reader something of the direct homely impression made by the original upon those for whom it was written." For the first time, modern English speakers found themselves hearing the

Scriptures in the kind of common idiom in which the earliest Greek and Hebrew readers of the Bible heard it.

Some critics even called Moffatt's version a translation of the Bible into Scottish. Moffatt listed a bagpipe among the musical instruments played as people bowed before King Nebuchadnezzar's image (Daniel 3:10), and he dressed David in a linen "kilt" as David danced before the Ark of the Covenant (2 Samuel 6:14). Other Scottish renderings included "yeomen" (Micah 2:2), "harts" (Lamentations 1:6), and the unforgettable phrase "I will hie me to your scented slopes" in Song of Songs 4:6.

Moffatt took other great liberties with the text, transposing whole passages in particular books from one place to another (see the repositioning of John 3:22-30 between 2:12 and 2:13) and completely deleting 1 Timothy 5:23, which says, "take a little wine for the sake of your stomach." All the same, Moffatt's Bible provided a refreshing model for future translations and helped to popularize an idiomatic approach to the translation process.

The British flavor of the English in some of these translations soon became a source of concern to Bible translators in the United States and Canada. Beginning in the 1920s, a number of translations by American and Canadian scholars appeared. The first of these was The Complete Bible: An American Translation, published in 1927 and revised in 1935 under the title The Bible: An American Translation.

Considered to be the American counterpart to Moffatt, The Complete Bible combined earlier translations of the New Testament by Edgar J. Goodspeed with Goodspeed's later translation of the Apocrypha and an Old Testament translation by J. M. Powis Smith. Smith was assisted in the Old Testament translation process by Theophile J. Meek of the University of Toronto, Alexander R. Gordon of McGill University, and Leroy Waterman of the University of Michigan.

In the original 1927 edition, Goodspeed and Smith describe their translation in this fashion: "It tries to be American in the sense that the writings of Lincoln, Roosevelt, and Wilson are American. This does not imply any limitation of our mother-tongue, but if anything an enrichment of it." Basing their work on the Greek text of Westcott and Hort (1881), the translators departed from the English of the KJV by omitting "thee," "thou," and "thy," except when referring to God. They also utilized small capital letters for LORD or GOD to indicate all references to Yahweh. Finally, they recovered the stylistic qualities of Hebrew poetry that had long been rendered as prose in English translations.

Two less popular American translations appeared shortly after the second edition of the Goodspeed/Smith translation. In 1937, Charles B. Williams of Union University in Jackson, Tennessee, published The New Testament: A Translation in the Language of the People. Williams's purpose was to use the "practical, every-day words" of "the cobbler and the cab-driver" and to replace the highly theological language used in most English translations and understood only by "the scholar" and "the minister." He insisted that "it is the thoughts of our New Testament, not its single words, that we have tried to translate." The translation is written in a flowing paragraph style with verse numbers superscripted and almost invisible. This translation was revised in 1950.

In 1945, Gerrit Verkuyl, Professor of New Testament at Princeton University, published the Berkeley Version of the New Testament, named for Berkeley, California, its place of publication. His purpose was to "bring us God's thoughts and ways" in "the language in which we think and live rather than that of our ancestors who expressed themselves differently."

A translation team of twenty scholars completed the Old Testament portion in 1959, and a joint edition was published. The Berkeley Bible is valuable for its extensive use of footnotes to clarify the text. It was revised in 1969 as The Modern Language Bible.

An excellent Catholic rendering of the New Testament from the Latin Vulgate into English also appeared in 1945. Ronald A. Knox, an Anglican convert to Catholicism and retired chaplain of Trinity College at Oxford, completed The New Testament in English at the insistence of Catholic officials in England and Wales. The version is published in paragraph form with verse numbers listed in the margins. Extensive and easily readable footnotes help to clarify difficult passages and include references to particular Greek manuscripts. Knox's rendering of the Old Testament appeared in 1949, and the entire Bible was published in 1955.

A number of other dynamic translations deserve special mention. Among these are Ferrar Fenton's The Holy Bible in Modern English (NT, 1895; entire Bible, 1903), which translates Genesis 1:1 as "By periods GOD created that which produced the Solar Systems; then that which produced the Earth," Richard G. Moulton's Modern Reader's Bible (1907), and William G. Ballantine's The Riverside New

Testament (1901; revised 1934). Also of interest are Clarence Jordan's editions of The Cotton Patch Version, published in the late-1960s and early 1970s, which translated not only the words of the Bible but also its setting. Jordan's translations of Paul's epistles, Luke and Acts, Matthew and John (eight chapters only), and the general Epistles are set in the American South.

General Idiomatic Translations

At the beginning of this chapter, we mentioned two different approaches to dynamic translation, the general idiomatic approach and the common language approach. Translators of the general idiomatic versions approached the text in a phrase-by-phrase translation style, making the text read as if it had been written in English. We now turn our attention to these general idiomatic translations.

The New Testament in Modern English (1958). In the 1940s, J. B. Phillips, a London pastor, undertook a translation of Paul's epistles, which eventually became part of one of the most popular dynamic English translations of the New Testament in the modern era. Phillips's interest in translating the Bible into contemporary English emerged from his parish work in London in 1941 when it occurred to him that the young people of his congregation, who were living in a bombed-out section of the city, might benefit from an easily readable account of the early church's struggle with persecution. He was particularly concerned that "these youngsters, who were by no means unintelligent, simply did not understand Bible language."

C. S. Lewis read Phillips's translation of Colossians in 1943, noting that "it was like seeing a familiar picture after it's been cleaned." This encouragement resulted in Phillips' Letters to Young Churches, a translation of all of Paul's epistles, which was published in 1947. Through the decade of the 1950s, he added the Gospels (1952), Acts (1955), and Revelation (1957). The entire New Testament was published in 1958, followed by a translation called The Four Prophets (Amos, Hosea, Isaiah 1–35, and Micah) in 1963, and a revision of the New Testament in 1972.

Phillips discussed his approach to translation in an autobiography, *The Price of Success*, published in 1984. His aim was to use commonly spoken English in an effort to produce a version that was easy to read. To this end, he first tried to clear his mind of the language of the King James Version. Then he developed a rough but accurate translation of the Greek into modern English without referring to any other translation. In the next stage, he ignored the Greek language completely and rewrote the rough translation into modern English. And finally, he compared his modern rewriting of the text with the original Greek. He consulted no other translations in the 1958 edition, though he corrected this obvious oversight in 1972.

Phillips's translation was well received and quite popular through the 1960s and 1970s for several reasons. It was printed with verse numbers only at the first line of each section, giving it a contemporary look. Section headings assisted the reader in finding familiar passages even without the verse numbers, though the headings are now somewhat dated. Consider the following examples: "Present Distress is Temporary and Negligible" and "To Partake of the Lord's Supper is a Supremely Serious Thing."

Most notably, Phillips utilized literary creativity in shaping the text. He tried "to imagine myself as each of the New Testament authors writing his particular message for the people of today." He hoped that this process would help him to capture Matthew's precision, Mark's bluntness, Luke's sympathetic nature, and John's mysticism. This imaginative approach alone makes his translation quite valuable among other twentieth-century English translations. It is important to note that the 1972 revision is a considerable improvement on the earlier edition. It used a better Greek text (1966 UBS text) and provided the occasion to respond to criticisms of the 1958 edition.

Several passages in the Phillips translation (1972 edition) accomplish his stated goal to bring clarity to the KJV text. He translates "my heart's desire" in Romans 10:1 as "from the bottom of my heart." He warms up the KJV of Romans 13:8 ("Owe no man any thing, but to love one another") with an encouragement to "Keep out of debt altogether, except that perpetual debt of love which we owe one another." His translation of Matthew 5:5 is perhaps the best translation ever of this often misunderstood beatitude: "Happy are those who claim nothing, for the whole earth will belong to them."

Other notable translations include the following passages:

Matthew 7:29—For his words had the ring of authority.

1 Corinthians 6:12—As a Christian, I may do anything, but that does not mean that everything is good for me. I may do everything, but I must not be a slave of anything.

2 Peter 2:17—These men are like wells without a drop of water in them, like the changing shapes of whirling storm-clouds, and their fate will be the black night of utter darkness.

Phillips's translation is a bit puzzling at certain points. Despite his effort to render a smooth reading in English, he occasionally lapses into an awkward literalism. Consider Matthew 8:26 and 14:31, in which the disciples and Peter are referred to as "you little-faiths" and "you little-faith" respectively. Here Phillips seems to abandon a smooth translation ("you of little faith") in an effort to express the exact Greek meaning of the text.

At other points, the translation becomes a bit too familiar for the context. In Matthew 27:40, as Jesus is crucified, the crowd mocks him with these words: "Hi, you who could pull down the Temple and build it up again in three days—why don't you save yourself," as if it were the most natural thing in the world to greet a dying man with a cheery "Hi"!

Two other weaknesses are apparent. The translation is quite gender exclusive with no attention paid to those points at which "men" might best be translated into an appropriately inclusive designation. Also, Phillips's use of difficult English words often hinders his goal of offering a translation that is easy to read. Consider the following examples: "palpable frauds" in Titus 1:16, "invidious distinctions" in James 2:9, "slightest prevarication" in 1 Peter 2:22, and "serried ranks of witnesses" in Hebrews 12:1.

Despite these inadequacies, Phillips offers a memorable translation, which is to be valued for its interpretation of particular passages (some of which are listed above) and for the equal weight it gives to both the needs of its readers and the concerns of the ancient writers. The translation is more than adequate as an aid to devotional study but quite ineffectual as a tool of scholarly inquiry and biblical exegesis.

The Jerusalem Bible (1966). The popularity of Phillips's translation spawned two new versions in the mid-1960s. One of these, Today's English Version, will be discussed with other common language translations. The other, the Jerusalem Bible, offered the first opportunity for English-speaking Catholics to read a translation of the Bible from the original languages that was also stamped with the imprimatur of the church. Both the Douay version of 1582 and Ronald Knox's translation in the 1940s were renderings from the Latin Vulgate.

A word of caution is in order. Though the JB is often described as an easily readable English translation from the ancient languages, in reality it is based quite extensively upon a French translation of the Bible called La Sainte Bible, completed between 1948 and 1954 by the French Dominicans of L'Ecole Biblique de Jerusalem in Israel.

The original French version contained extensive notes and commentary in several volumes. But this was subsequently reduced to a single volume in 1956. Some ten years later, Alexander Jones of Christ's College in Liverpool, England, directed Roman Catholic scholars in an English translation of this one-volume abridgment of the original French work.

The extent to which the English translation borrowed from its French counterpart is of great concern to biblical scholars. The foreword acknowledges that "in the case of a few books the initial draft was made from the French and was then compared word for word with the Hebrew or Aramaic." But it goes on to insist that "for the much greater part, the initial drafts were made from the Hebrew or Greek and simultaneously compared with the French. . . ."

The edition of 1966 included the voluminous notes of the one-volume French translation. It also contained a number of helpful tables and maps in the appendices. In addition, it followed the Christian or Catholic canon by including the deuterocanonical or apocryphal books (Tobit, Judith, 1 and 2 Maccabees, Wisdom, Ecclesiasticus, and additions to Daniel and Esther) in their original canonical place, and not grouped together between the testaments.

This translation goes to great lengths to appeal to readers outside the Catholic faith. In fact, many Protestants are hardly aware of its Catholic flavor. This is especially true of the 1968 Reader's Edition, published in paperback, which is probably the version with which most people are familiar. Perhaps the most helpful feature for Protestant readers of both editions is that biblical names are printed in the form found in the RSV. While Catholic doctrinal positions were certainly spelled out in the extensive notes of the 1966 edition, these comments were removed from the 1968 version. One Catholic peculiarity that sometimes confounds Protestants is the use of the word *holocaust* in the place of "burnt offerings." The end result, however, is a translation that has found an extensive and appreciative audience in Protestant churches.

Literary luminaries such as J. R. R. Tolkien and Robert Speaight had a hand in shaping the English language in the Jerusalem Bible. Perhaps this is why it has been praised for its powerful language and effective storytelling. Its translation of Philippians 2:5-11 is perhaps the best example of this simplicity and literary power:

> His state was divine,
> yet he did not cling
> to his equality with God
> but emptied himself
> to assume the condition of a slave,
> and became as men are;
> and being as all men are,
> he was humbler yet,
> even to accepting death,
> death on a cross.
> But God raised him high
> and gave him the name
> which is above all other names
> so that all beings
> in the heavens, on earth and in the underworld,
> should bend the knee at the name of Jesus
> and that every tongue should acclaim
> Jesus Christ as Lord,
> to the glory of God the Father.

The JB has been criticized in a number of areas. It fails to provide modern equivalents for monetary and weight designations in the ancient world. It alone among all modern translations pluralizes the word *grace* in 1 Corinthians 1:4: "I never stop thanking God for all the *graces* you have received through Jesus Christ." In a rather glaring oversight, it omits "in one body" from 1 Corinthians 12:13, a construction that is obviously present.

The JB is much more traditional in its translation philosophy than the Phillips. It appears that its innovative place in Catholic biblical scholarship caused its translators to err on the side of a traditional reading. For this reason, it is probably a more valuable exegetical tool than is Phillips' translation. However, the serious Bible student will want to secure a copy of the original 1966 edition in order to take full advantage of the helpful notes and other supplements.

The New English Bible (1970). The NEB is the result of a proposal at the 1946 General Assembly of the Church of Scotland to undertake a completely new English translation of the Bible, which would be outside the tradition of the Authorized Version. A joint committee to direct the translation process was appointed in 1947 and headed by J. W. Trunkin, Bishop of Truro. Members of the committee included representatives of the Church of England, the Church of Scotland, the Methodist, Baptist, and Congregationalist denominations, Oxford and Cambridge University Presses, and several Bible societies. Roman Catholics were later invited to participate as observers.

The joint committee appointed three panels of translators (one each for the Old and New Testaments and the Apocrypha) and a panel for stylistic and literary concerns. These panels followed a carefully prescribed translation process. First, an individual translator prepared a first translation draft of each book. This draft was then forwarded to members of the appropriate panel for revision. Members of the literary/stylistic panel then reviewed the revision and suggested changes to improve the literary quality of the translation. These suggestions were either accepted or rejected by the translation panel. Finally, the entire book was submitted to the joint committee for final approval.

The translation team had at least three audiences in mind. It hoped to appeal to those people who rarely frequented church and were put off by the stately English of the AV. It was also intended for young people who wanted a more contemporary translation and for churchgoers who had become overly familiar with the text of the AV. The translation was intended to "be genuinely English in idiom, such as will not awaken a sense of strangeness or remoteness." It aimed for a "timeless English," which would be neither archaic in tone nor too colloquial, so that the translation might not only survive but also possess "sufficient dignity to be read aloud."

The New Testament translation, published in 1961 by Oxford and Cambridge Presses, quickly became a best-seller, as did the entire Bible upon its publication in 1970. A slight revision was issued in 1972. The bulk of credit for the translation must go to C. H. Dodd, director of the project from its inception, and to J. W. Hunkin, A. T. P.

Williams, and F. D. Coggan, who each chaired the joint committee at various stages in the lengthy translation process.

A number of criticisms were leveled against the NEB because it was perceived to be an intentional effort to replace the AV. No less a literary authority than T. S. Eliot is reported to have said of it, "So long as the New English Bible was used only for private reading, it would be merely a symptom of the decay of the English language. . . . But the more it is adopted for religious services the more it will become an active agent of decadence."

One apparent weakness of the NEB is also its greatest strength. Most scholarly criticism of the translation can be traced to a bold decision on the part of the New Testament translation panel to develop its own Greek text. The panel decided to use that Greek manuscript which, in its estimation, best reflected the original words of the ancient writer in each passage. This new "eclectic" Greek text, created in the process of translation, was then published in 1964 by R. V. G. Tasker. Its use in translation led to some significant renderings of the Greek and Hebrew, and some problematic interpretations.

The following verses are made much more clear in the NEB:

> Exodus 10:27—The Lord made Pharaoh obstinate, and he refused to let them go. 'Out! Pester me no more!' he said to Moses.

> Mark 5:14—The men in charge of them took to their heels.

> John 1:1—When all things began, the Word already was. The Word dwelt with God, and what God was, the Word was.

Some reordering of verses occurs as a result of the use of an eclectic Greek text. Genesis 26:18 is placed between verses 15 and 16. Matthew 9:34 is completely dropped, as is Jeremiah 15:13-14, which is relegated to a footnote.

In several places throughout the translation, the translators added short phrases that inappropriately shade the meaning of the text. These problematic translations include Genesis 1:1, which takes considerable license when it adds the words "of creation" to "In the beginning." John 1:12 is translated "But to all who did receive him, to those who have yielded him their allegiance, he gave the right to become children of God," as if "yielded . . . allegiance" and "believed in his name" had the same shade of meaning. In Romans 5:14 the translators added the phrase "by disobeying a direct command" to clarify the nature of Adam's sin.

The British flavor of the translation is obvious throughout the text, with British spellings and references to British forms of currency. For a translation that set out to use contemporary English, the NEB is replete with old-style Britishisms. Consider: "foregather" (Job 1:4), "panniers" (Job 5:5), "batten" (Proverbs 5:10), and "bedizened" (Revelation 18:17). Perhaps it is a Britishism that leads to the rather humorous translation of 1 Corinthians 5:9: "I wrote to you that you must have nothing to do with loose livers."

The NEB is a text for scholars, particularly those who are attracted to its innovative use of a self-determined Greek text. At the same time, its readers should be warned that its unique Greek text is certainly not utilized by most other translations and so the NEB should be used with caution. Its translation philosophy is traditional enough to warrant use by serious students of the Bible, and the style of its English is formal enough for public reading.

The Revised English Bible (1989). A revision of the NEB was published in 1989 as the Revised English Bible (REB). This revision process began as early as 1974 when the joint committee responsible for the NEB approved this major revision of the text. A number of new member denominations and societies were added to the joint committee, including the Roman Catholic Church, the United Reformed Church, the Moravian Church, and the Salvation Army. REB translators followed much the same process as their NEB forebears, dividing the group into panels to translate the Old Testament, New Testament, and Apocrypha respectively. They departed from their predecessors' use of an eclectic Greek text, however, preferring the 1979 Nestle-Aland Novum Testamentum Graece.

Several quite obvious changes were made in the new edition. God is addressed in the REB with the less formal "you" rather than "thou." Some effort is made to alter the use of gender-exclusive language, though such changes are quite minimal and sporadic for a translation of the period of the late 1980s. The translation remains quite free of subheadings, at least when compared to other versions, though the REB panels have added a number of new ones. The REB departs from its predecessor with its two columns and quite traditional style, which significantly alters the NEB's rather booklike and quite innovative appearance. Finally, considerable effort was put into reducing the British flavor of the NEB.

The REB received extensive accolades for its readability. It effectively modernizes the English of the NEB, which was already generally accepted as a translation for public reading. The beatitudes of Matthew 5 express this significant improvement. The phrase "How blest are those" is replaced by the more simple "Blessed" so that, in 5:3, "How blest are those who know their need of God" (NEB) becomes "Blessed are the poor in spirit" (REB). The opening prologue to John receives similar attention. The NEB translated John 1:1 as "When all things began, the Word already was. The Word dwelt with God, and what God was, the Word was." The REB offers a much improved version: "In the beginning, the Word already was. The Word was in God's presence, and what God was, the Word was."

Psalm 23 in the REB offers another example of the translation's beauty and readability. The phrase "I shall want nothing" in the NEB is changed to "I lack for nothing." "And leads me beside the waters of peace" becomes "he leads me to water where I may rest." Unfortunately, the REB retains two rather awkward NEB renderings in Psalm 23, specifically, "your shepherd's staff and crook afford me comfort" and the phrase "throughout the years to come," which the NEB had translated as "my whole life long."

Several other awkward translations reappear in the REB, including Proverbs 19:29 ("There is a rod in pickle for the arrogant") and Song of Songs 1:7 ("that I may not be left picking lice as I sit among your companion's herds"). Neither the NEB nor the REB offers much in the way of notes to assist the reader in understanding such difficult passages or to explain their use of a verse translation that so obviously deviates from more traditional renderings.

The REB has been roundly criticized for its sporadic and quite limited use of gender-inclusive language, especially since one of its stated purposes was to avoid male-oriented language. To their credit, the translators changed "man" in Genesis 1:26 and "mankind" in Genesis 6:1 to "human beings" and "the human race" respectively. This gender-inclusive approach is retained in verses such as Psalm 1:1 ("Happy is the one"), John 7:53 ("they all went home" as over against "each to his home"), and various other passages.

But the REB then reverts to male-specific language in Matthew 4 and Luke 4 ("Man is not to live on bread alone"), John 12:25 ("Whoever loves himself is lost, but he who hates himself in this world will be kept safe for eternal life"), Acts 17:26 ("He created from one stock every nation of men"), and numerous other passages. No rationale for the use of gender-specific language is stated in the preface. Morna Hooker, a female scholar who served on the New Testament translation panel, defends the translation by pointing out that the biblical writers "lived in a patriarchal society, and we cannot comprehend what they were trying to say unless we accept that fact."

The REB stands as a worthy successor to the NEB, particularly as a source for scholarly study of the use of texts in Bible translations and as a readable version for use in public worship. Its rather awkward effort to move toward more gender-inclusive language enables it to serve as a bridge between those translations of the past that completely ignored such concerns and those translations of the future that will ignore such issues at their peril.

The New Century Version (1991). The New Century Version has a unique beginning, emerging out of a decision by the World Bible Translation Center to create a Bible for the hearing-impaired. The simplicity and readability of this first version led to the translation of the International Children's Bible (ICB), a forerunner to the NCV, by a team of twenty scholars representing a cross section of conservative, evangelical, and Protestant denominations. Significantly, several members of the translation team had served as translators for the NASB, NIV, NKJV, and RSV. No woman translator was included on the team.

The New Testament translation of the ICB was released in 1983, followed by the entire Bible in 1986. A number of guidelines directed the translation effort. Its readability was to be on about a third-grade level. This goal was achieved by limiting vocabulary to the *Living Word Vocabulary*, a reference guide utilized in the preparation of *World Book Encyclopedia*. The translators also avoided long sentences, used modern weight designations, and maintained consistent and familiar use of place-names.

The ICB was enthusiastically greeted by conservative evangelical leaders such as James Dobson, who declared, "We've looked for a trustworthy translation for children; and now we've found it." But representatives of mainline denominations were troubled by the anti-Jewish rhetoric that pervaded the translation. William Willimon of The United Methodist Church pointed out that where the KJV had translated John 11:53 as "Then from that day forth they took counsel together for to put him to death," the ICB rendered it "That day the Jewish leaders started planning to kill him." Even more troubling were the ICB subheadings, which included interpretive phrases, such as "Jewish Leaders Try to Trap Jesus," "The Jews Try to Arrest Jesus," and "The Jews Against Jesus." In later revisions, these phrases were changed to correct the anti-Jewish flavor.

The success of the ICB inspired an edition for adults, called the New Century Version, which was published in 1991. A new translation team was appointed, since this new version would have a much different target audience. Among the translators were biblical scholars from across the spectrum of evangelical Protestantism, representing a number of conservative seminaries and colleges, including Denver Baptist Conservative Seminary, Fuller Theological Seminary, Gordon-Conwell Theological Seminary, Columbia Bible College, Dallas Theological Seminary, Wheaton College, and Trinity Evangelical Seminary. The lone woman on the translation team was Margaret Bratcher of Mercer University.

According to a promotional brochure released by its publisher, Word Publishing Company of Dallas, Texas, this new translation was to be "accurate, free of denominational bias, and clear to the broadest possible English-speaking audience." The preface to the NCV states that its translators "recognize that the most accurate translations are those which pay close attention to the meanings of words in their broader context, rather than those which simply treat words as isolated entities."

Several principles guided the translation. Like the ICB, the NCV took as its vocabulary base *The Living Word Vocabulary* used by *The World Book Encyclopedia*. Modern equivalents for currency, weights, and measures were substituted for their ancient counterparts. Confusion over place-names was resolved by using only the most familiar name for a geographical location (for example, Lake Galilee in the place of Lake Gennesaret or Sea of Tiberias). The meanings behind ancient customs were clarified, as were the meanings of words whose usage in English had changed in recent years (for example, *devote* is rendered "destroyed as an offering to the Lord"). The NCV also made every effort to use gender-inclusive language when such language preserved the original meaning of the text.

The clarity of the NCV, as well as its use of gender-inclusive language, is evident in its translation of Psalm 8:4—"But why are people important to you? Why do you take care of human beings?" Its rendering of Matthew 4:4 (see also Luke 4:4) is equally refreshing: "A person does not live by eating only bread, but by everything God says."

The NCV contains a number of fresh interpretations, for which it is ranked among the clearest English translations available today. Consider the following passages:

> Genesis 3:17—So I will put a curse on the ground, and you will have to work very hard for your food.

> Psalm 23:1–3—The Lord is my shepherd; I have everything I need. He lets me rest in green pastures. He leads me to calm water. He gives me new strength.

The use of a limited vocabulary occasionally detracts from the beauty of the translation. Genesis 1:1 is translated "In the beginning God created the sky and the earth" which certainly does not carry the aesthetic power of the more traditional "heavens." The beatitudes in Matthew 5 may suffer more than any other passage as a result of this limitation:

> Those people who know they have great spiritual needs are
>   happy, because the kingdom of heaven belongs to them.
> Those who are sad now are happy, because God will
>   comfort them.
> Those who are humble are happy, because the earth will
>   belong to them.

Finally, the effort to create a clear translation is sometimes hindered by improper sentence construction such as that found in Psalm 23:3*b*: "He leads me on paths that are right for the good of his name."

The NCV is a clear and concise translation that is helpful to both the serious Bible scholar and the devotional reader. It is to be commended for its use of gender-inclusive language, despite the limitation of a predominantly male translation team. Unfortunately, it should always be viewed with a healthy suspicion by those Christian traditions outside of conservative and Protestant evangelicalism who had no hand in its translation.

New Living Translation (1996). In July 1996, a fresh new translation of the Scriptures hit bookstore shelves. Encased in a contemporary cover designed to attract customer attention, the New Living Translation touts itself as "Easy to Understand" and "Relevant for Today." Tyndale House, the NLT's publisher, launched the translation with an initial printing of 950,000 copies and a $2.5 million publicity budget. It also has its own web site on the Internet, an indication that its promoters intend for it to be a major player among Bible translations well into the next century.

The NLT team of some ninety translation specialists had two primary goals. First, they wanted to revise and update Kenneth Taylor's popular 1970s Bible paraphrase, *The Living Bible,* by checking Taylor's work against the ancient languages. Second, and perhaps more important, they hoped to fashion a new dynamic translation of the Bible that would stand on its own.

The translation team consisted of scholars from a wide range of conservative, evangelical, and Protestant seminaries and colleges, including a few from England and Australia. The team included in its ranks a number of Pentecostals, Mennonites, Baptists, conservative Methodists and Presbyterians, independent evangelicals, and members of several other traditions.

The purpose of the NLT is "to be both exegetically accurate and idiomatically powerful." To accomplish this objective, the Bible Translation Committee appointed three scholars to each book of the Bible. Each scholar then reviewed the assigned book (in the LB) and proposed first-draft revisions. The draft fashioned by the three scholars was then taken through several stages of exegetical and stylistic revision and reviewed and approved by the Bible Translation Committee. The translation team used the Masoretic Text of the Biblia Hebraica Stuttgartensia of 1977 as the basis for its Old Testament translation. New Testament translators utilized both the UBS's 1993 Greek New Testament text and the 1993 Nestle-Aland Novum Testamentum Graece.

The translators followed a number of guidelines that were intended to make the text more readable. Ancient weights and measures were converted to modern American equivalents. Ancient currency was identified according to its approximate weight in precious metals, a designation that can hardly be expected to eliminate confusion. Time designations are updated to approximate modern equivalents either by references to seasons or actual dates when possible. Idiomatic expressions are translated into their closest modern English equivalent. Metaphorical language is generally maintained, though an effort is made to assist the reader to understand the meaning of the metaphor. For example, the phrase "Your neck is like the tower of David" is translated as "Your neck is as stately as the tower of David." The translation makes every effort to be gender inclusive.

Several kinds of footnotes are provided to clarify the text. These notes identify references to Old Testament passages, cultural and historical information, textual variants, the meanings of proper names, transliterations of place-names, and alternative renderings.

A Tyndale Bible "verse finder," placed at the beginning of the translation, clearly betrays the conservatism of the translation. The first entry directs the reader's attention to verses that condemn "Abortion," no small feat given the fact that no direct reference to such a practice exists in the Bible. "Homosexuality" is roundly condemned, though "Divorce" is not even listed. Interestingly enough, four verses are listed under the category of "Women." None of the summary phrases or the verses indicated are concerned with the subjugation of women to men. Genesis 1:26-27 is introduced with the phrase "God's image is shared equally by women and men." Galatians 3:28 is summarized by the statement that "women and men are equal before God."

Perhaps the best place to begin analyzing the NLT is by comparing it to its parent version, *The Living Bible*. Significant changes have been made throughout the new translation. The most infamous verse in the LB is Saul's curse of Jonathan in 1 Samuel 20:30 ("You son of a bitch!"). Conservative critique of this interpretation led to the following revision in the NLT: "You stupid son of a whore." Both versions contain a footnote that indicates that the original Hebrew reads, "You son of a perverse and rebellious woman."

A comparison of Genesis 1 in the two versions draws attention to the effort by NLT translators to fashion a translation that is more closely aligned with the ancient languages. Genesis 1:1 in the LB is rendered "When God began creating the heavens and the earth, ..." The NLT reads much like a more formal translation: "In the beginning God created the heavens and the earth." Verse 3 in the NLT substitutes "and there was light" for the LB's "And light appeared."

Psalm 23 offers another interesting comparison. Verses 133 in the LB contain the following free interpretation: "Because the Lord is my Shepherd, I have everything I need! He lets me rest in the meadow grass and leads me beside the quiet streams. He restores my failing health. He helps me do what honors him the most."

The NLT is again much more in keeping with traditional translations: "The Lord is my shepherd; I have everything I need. He lets me rest in green meadows; he leads me beside peaceful streams. He renews my strength. He guides me along right paths, bringing honor to his name."

The NLT translation of the beatitudes in Matthew 5 is among the best offered by dynamic translations. Each beatitude begins with the phrase "God blesses those. . ." Matthew 5:1 is translated "God blesses those who realize their need for him, for the Kingdom of Heaven is given to them." This is a considerable improvement on the LB's rather poor paraphrase, which even introduces gender exclusivity into the verse: "'Humble men are very fortunate!' He told them, 'for the Kingdom of Heaven is given to them.'"

The NLT claims to be the "first adult-level Bible translated by evangelical scholars using the dynamic-equivalence (thought-for-thought) method of translation." Indeed, it is written on a sixth-grade reading level, which is considerably higher than the reading level of either the NCV or the CEV. It contains sentences of greater length and complexity than either of these two other translations. For this reason, it will find a receptive audience among adults who find themselves torn between the flow of verbal translations like the NIV or the NKJV and the simplicity of the NCV or CEV.

Common Language Versions

A number of common language versions have appeared in recent years. The translators of these versions believe that it is not enough to develop a few simple rules of thumb to assist the translation process. Rather, the translator must fully understand the formal structure of both the source language (original language) and the receptor language (language of the new translation) in order to fashion a clear and accurate translation.

This process has been compared to the task of transferring the contents of a wide-bodied freight train to a narrow-bodied train. The transfer necessitates the use of more cars and of placing a different volume of cargo in each car. The end result should be the same. The cargo will arrive at its destination. For translators then, the task is to utilize whatever number of words and images is necessary in the receptor language to communicate the original meaning of the source language.

Good News Bible: Today's English Version (1976). The first translation to take such concerns seriously was the Good News Bible, published, surprisingly enough, by the American Bible Society, which had previously printed only verbal translations such as the KJV and the RSV. According to Eugene Nida, whose translation philosophy guided the project, the GNB/TEV had its genesis in the success of a common language Spanish translation in the late 1950s which was directed toward millions of Indians living in areas from northern Mexico to southern Chile. Nida notes that this Spanish version "was not a patronizing, stripped down version of the scriptures, but one which used the common language of the vast majority of Spanish-speaking people."

The decision was quickly made by the ABS to publish a similar English translation. A sample translation of Mark's gospel was prepared under the direction of Robert G. Bratcher, a former Southern Baptist missionary to Brazil. The enthusiastic response to this volume encouraged the Society to ask Bratcher to translate the entire New Testament.

Bratcher's translation was published in 1966 under the title Good News for Modern Man. Based upon the UBS's The Greek New Testament, this version quickly sold some twelve million copies. An Old Testament translation was then undertaken by a team of seven translators, most of whom had already assisted in the process of Bible translation in international mission contexts. A member of the British and Foreign Bible Society advised on matters of British usage and assisted in the preparation of a British edition. The translation team used the *Masoretic Text*, edited by Rudolf Kittel, as its Hebrew text.

The complete Bible was then published in 1976 as *Good News Bible: The Bible in Today's English Version*. This 1976 edition offered the opportunity for some significant revisions to three earlier New Testament editions as well as to several Old Testament books that had been separately published between 1970 and 1976. To the editors' credit, careful attention was paid in this first full edition to verse translations or subheadings that had been deemed by critics of the earlier editions as too anti-Semitic in tone. For example, "the Jews" of John 11:53 in the earlier edition became "the Jewish authorities."

Several guidelines were adopted by the translation team. Although no vocabulary limitations were placed upon the translation, the language of the GNB was intended to be "natural, clear, simple, and unambiguous." Names of persons and places were printed in their most familiar form. Yahweh (YHWH) is translated as simply "Lord."

Extensive reader's notes supplemented the text, including cultural and historical notes, textual notes, alternative renderings, and references to other passages. Short introductions to each book were included, as well as a short outline. The appendices consisted of a word list, chronological chart of major biblical events, an index, Septuagint passages, and maps.

Perhaps the most distinctive feature of the GNB is its line drawings, which drew mixed reviews. These were prepared by Annie Valloton, a Swiss artist, and were intended to draw the reader into the text. The drawings were intentionally timeless and bridged the gap between the ancient and contemporary worlds. They helped to tell biblical stories as well as to express abstract theological concepts in concrete form. In the drawing for 1 John 4:15 ("Perfect love drives out all fear") one human being is standing erect with outstretched arms while three other forms cower in fear.

The GNB is an accurate and carefully constructed translation that usually succeeds in capturing the idiomatic flavor of the ancient Greek and Hebrew. Consider the following examples:

> Genesis 1:1-2—In the beginning, when God created the universe, the earth was formless and desolate. The raging ocean that covered everything was engulfed in total darkness, and the power of God was moving over the water.

> Genesis 2:1—And so the whole universe was completed.

> Psalm 23:1-3—The Lord is my shepherd; I have everything I need. He lets me rest in fields of green grass and leads me to quiet pools of fresh water. He gives me new strength. He guides me in the right paths, as he has promised.

> John 1:1—Before the world was created, the Word already existed; he was with God, and he was the same as God. From the very beginning the Word was with God.

W. F. Stinespring has praised the GNB for its translation of Ecclesiastes 3:1-2—"Everything that happens in this world happens at the time God chooses. He sets the time for birth and the time for death, . . ." In his estimation, the GNB succeeds where other versions have failed because it captures the true sense of the active Hebrew verb rather than rendering it in the traditional passive construction, "There is a time. . . ."

Careful pains are taken to modernize words such as *centurion,* *Publicans, Sanhedrin, raca, mammon,* and many other terms. Theological concepts like "justify" are translated into simple phrases such as "put right with God."

The GNB can be roundly criticized in at least two areas. First, it oversimplifies certain complex passages. The Song of Songs, for example, which is one of the most difficult of all biblical books, reads in the GNB like a simple little love story. Its rendering of 8:6 ("Close your heart to every love but mine; hold no one in your arms but me") is certainly a mere shadow of the NRSV's "Set me as a seal upon your heart, as a seal upon your arm; for love is strong as death, passion fierce as the grave." And the beatitudes in Matthew 5 suffer from the repetition of the word *Happy* at the beginning of each phrase.

Second, like the REB, it is rather cavalier in its attention to gender-inclusive language. Perhaps 1976 is a bit early to expect such sensitivity, but it is important to point out such weaknesses for those who may find this gender exclusion distracting or even offensive. Genesis 1:26 is translated, "And now we will make human beings. . . ." But Genesis 6:1 returns to the gender-specific "mankind" and adds insult to injury with a chapter heading that draws attention to "The Wickedness of Mankind." Psalm 1:1 warns against "evil men." Psalm 8:4 asks the question, "What is man, that you think of him; mere man, that you care for him?" In Matthew 4:4, Jesus quotes Deuteronomy, "Man cannot live on bread alone."

While the GNB was adequate for its day, it now suffers from the very fate that its earliest reviewers predicted. Its brand of common English is quickly becoming dated. Nowhere is this more obvious than in its use of gender-exclusive language. In addition, its line drawings, while certainly innovative when it was first released, now seem somewhat old-fashioned and stylistically dated.

The Contemporary English Version (1995). Fortunately, the American Bible Society has not rested on its laurels. It has prepared a new translation, The Contemporary English Version, which is a worthy successor to its older sibling. The CEV began in the mind of Barclay Newman, who had assisted in the translation of the GNB. In the mid-1980s, Newman began to study popular forms of the English language found in books, magazines, newspapers, and the television, to see what kind of language people were speaking and hearing. He was particularly concerned with how people heard texts when they were being read aloud.

In 1986 he published a "test" volume that was a collection of illustrated Scripture passages for children. Its warm public reception encouraged Newman to translate the entire Bible. The New Testament was completed on the 175th anniversary of the American Bible Society in 1991. The entire Bible was published in 1995.

The CEV claims to be a translation in the philosophical tradition of the King James Bible, which the CEV preface describes as "the most important document in the history of the English language." Like the translators of the KJV, the CEV translation team hoped to produce "a text that is faithful to the meaning of the original." The CEV utilized the text of the UBS's Biblia Hebraica Stuttgartensia for the Old Testament portion and the UBS's Greek New Testament (third edition) for the New Testament portion.

The effect of public reading of the Bible was a primary concern of the CEV translators. To this end, three guiding principles shaped the translation. First, it should be easy for an inexperienced reader to read aloud without stumbling. Since most readers usually pause at the end of a line, attention was paid to line breaks in the text in order to reduce the possibility of misunderstanding on the part of the hearer. Second, it should be understood by someone with little familiarity with biblical language. And third, it should be understood and enjoyed by English speakers regardless of their religious or educational background.

The CEV makes every effort at gender-inclusive language except in the case of references to God. Genesis 1:26 ("humans") and 6:1 ("More and more people were born") provide examples of the careful and systematic use of such language throughout the translation.

Like the GNB, the CEV makes every effort to rid itself of complex theological language and "biblicisms." Words such as *righteousness, redemption, atonement,* and *sanctification* are avoided in favor of simple phrases that express the same theological truth but in a much clearer fashion. Also, the translators paid careful attention to sentences that might be unfamiliar to those persons with little experience in reading the Bible. Stephen's rebuke in Acts 7:51 ("You stiff-necked people, with uncircumcised hearts and ears!") is rendered "You stubborn and hardheaded people!" In a similar way, "those who had fallen asleep in him" (1 Thessalonians 4:14) is translated "his followers who have already died."

The removal of theological verbiage is perhaps the greatest contribution of the translation. The NIV has translated Romans 3:21 in the following way: "But now a righteousness from God, apart from the law, has been made known, to which the law and the prophets testify." The CEV offers an alternative translation that is much more accessible: "Now we see how God does make us acceptable to him. The Law and the Prophets tell how we become acceptable, and it isn't by obeying the Law of Moses." This simplification of abstract theological terms occurs time and again throughout the CEV, and particularly in Pauline literature.

This attempt to remove theological language and "biblicisms" does not always succeed. Certain passages suffer in the translation. This is particularly true of the creation story in Genesis 1. In Genesis 1:3, God says "'I command light to shine!' And light started shining," which is a far cry from the more familiar and stately, "And God said, 'Let there be light.' And there was light." The simple phrase "And it was so" is replaced by "And that's what happened." Also, in verse 27, God says "Have a lot of children," which is certainly a poor replacement for the more regal "Be fruitful and multiply." People who frequently read the Bible will find other instances in which the translation seems inadequate.

For the most part, though, the CEV accomplishes its goal of offering a readable common language translation of the Bible that is free of theological jargon. Such an accomplishment is important in a time of rising illiteracy. The CEV places in the hands of the public a Bible translation that is beautiful in its simplicity and, more important, easily read and understood.

Paraphrases

Considerable debate has raged in recent years over the value of paraphrased versions of the Bible. This debate centers around the very nature of the translation process itself. In many ways, all translations are paraphrases of the Bible, because no translation can ever capture the exact meaning of the original language. Certainly all general idiomatic and common language translations of the Bible paraphrase the text somewhat as the translators seek to find idioms in the receptor language with meanings similar to idioms in the source language.

Perhaps the whole debate is simply a matter of degree. Certain Bible versions are more concerned with communicating spiritual truth in everyday English than with remaining faithful to the exact meaning of the original language. These versions are best described as paraphrases. Unlike verbal and dynamic translations, paraphrases hope to express the spiritual truths of the Bible in something like the way the original authors would have done had they been writing in English. A paraphrase is not to be considered inferior to a verbal or dynamic translation. In fact, Robert C. Bowman has said that "sometimes accuracy may be found on the side of a paraphrase and sometimes on the side of a literal translation."

Two popular paraphrased versions of the Bible have been published in the late twentieth century. We have already introduced *The Living Bible* in our discussion of its descendant, the NLT. Without doubt, the LB dramatically transformed the popular view of the Bible upon its publication in 1971. A second paraphrase, entitled *The Message*, received an enthusiastic response when it was published by NavPress in 1993.

The Living Bible (1971)

We both remember the revival of interest in the Bible spawned by the publication of the LB in the early 1970s. As young teenagers, we sat in church and passed the time by reading the LB. Its words opened up a new perspective on biblical stories, making them seem relevant to a whole generation of American youth. Always we were aware of the controversy surrounding it. The LB was, after all, a "paraphrase," which, based upon the tone in which the word was spoken by our pastors, made it seem somehow "unclean" and therefore highly attractive to American young people.

Many people loved it. In 1972 it was the best-selling nonfiction book in America. By October 1973 it was in its thirty-third printing. Pat Boone called it "the single most important contribution America has made to the world." Many people attributed their conversion to Christianity to the power of its words. Twenty million copies had been sold by 1979.

But not everyone praised it. One newspaper columnist asked, "Can you imagine any English professor urging a modernized version of Shakespeare to meet the modern hippie vocabulary?" Carl McIntire dubbed it "the worst of all the different new Bibles that have been produced." People were disturbed by its straightforward sexual language such as that found in Genesis 4:1—"Then Adam had sexual intercourse with Eve his wife, and she conceived and gave birth to a son." One reviewer was appalled! "Does this mean," he asked, "that every time a baby is born in the Bible we have to explain to a child how it was done?"

At the center of this storm was Kenneth N. Taylor, a seminary-trained publisher, whose concern that the ASV of 1901 was unintelligible to most Americans led him to undertake this revision of the English Bible. Like J. B. Phillips before him, Taylor began work on the paraphrase in order to help his ten children understand the Bible. He hoped to restate the authors' thoughts "in different words than the author used" and to do so from a "rigid evangelical position."

The LB never claimed to be anything other than a paraphrase, though a team of Greek and Hebrew "experts" did make a careful scrutiny of the text to check content. Taylor goes so far as to point out that "there are dangers in paraphrases, as well as values." And the danger is "that the translator, however honest, may be giving the English reader something that the original writer did not mean to say." Taylor's goal was to "simplify the complex words of the Bible" in order to deepen the spiritual lives of his readers and to make it "easier for them to follow their Lord."

One must certainly approach the LB with considerable caution. To what extent is its "rigid evangelical position" read into the text and to what extent does that position emerge out of the text? And, perhaps more important, shouldn't one make every effort to read the Bible on its own terms rather than through a particular theological lens?

Taylor's "rigid evangelicalism" (read "Fundamentalism") is clearly evident in passages such as Galatians 5:11, Ephesians 3:21, and 1 Timothy 2:7 in which he uses the obviously evangelical phrase "plan of salvation" in the place of phrases such as "the offense of the cross" and "the true faith." Romans 1:16 raises similar concerns. Taylor replaces "salvation" with "bringing all who believe to heaven." Certainly this is the common perception of salvation among "rigid evangelicals" but it may be somewhat misleading when it restricts the word to this other worldly focus.

Another concern is that Taylor sometimes diminishes the humanity of Jesus in favor of a strengthened divinity. For example, the phrase "I, the Messiah" is substituted for Jesus' description of himself as "Son of Man." This is especially troublesome in Mark's gospel, in which Jesus often downplays his divinity.

Other kinds of textual manipulation also occur. Second Samuel 21:19 has always caused problems for biblical inerrantists because it identifies Elhanan, son of Jaare-Oregim, and not David, as the man who killed Goliath the Gittite. Taylor nicely fixes this problem by identifying Elhanan as the killer of "the *brother* of Goliath the Gittite." One wonders how many other passages were altered to make all the Bible's stories correspond.

Does this mean that the LB should be avoided? Not at all. Taylor is to be praised for this successful effort, which, more than any other event, may be responsible for the Bible's wide popularity today. He is also to be commended for his early decision to set up a missionary foundation to receive the royalties from the LB. In addition, the success of the LB has enabled him to establish Tyndale House Publishers as a major force in the Christian publishing industry.

The Message (1993)

In 1993 Eugene Peterson's *The Message* hit bookstore shelves and quickly became a popular Bible version, especially among the younger generation. Peterson, a Presbyterian pastor, had published a number of books in the area of Christian spirituality before turning his attention to the Bible. He describes himself as a pastor at heart, whose chief concern in life is to devote himself to his parishioners.

The Message, a paraphrase of the New Testament, reminds one of J. B. Phillips's The New Testament in Modern English. It contains neither verse numbers nor the usual two-column standard biblical format. Its purpose is to recapture the vitality and power with which the Bible was first heard by ancient peoples. Peterson points out that the Bible was written in informal Greek, "the street language of the day, the idiom of the playground and the marketplace."

For this reason, he believes it should be rendered into English "not as a refined language that appeals to our aspirations after the best but a rough and earthy language that captures God's presence and action where we least expect it." Peterson hoped to capture in his Bible the tone of everyday English, which is equally at home discussing world events and the day's shopping. He points out that as a pastor he has always stood at the intersection of two languages, serving as an interpreter and translator so that "men and women . . . could find their way around and get along in this world where God has spoken so decisively and clearly in Jesus."

The Message is free of any study aids or notes to assist in the interpretation of the text; the Bible appears readily accessible to its readers. A short introduction is provided at the beginning of each New Testament book.

Like the LB, *The Message* must be approached with some caution. It is apparently free of the obvious theological bias that characterizes the LB, though translators cannot help but import their own perspectives into the text. Peterson's interest in spirituality is obvious since the text reads almost like a spiritual treatise that might have been written by an early church father or mother.

Its greatest fault is that it is a paraphrase. On many occasions Peterson adds short phrases to clear up confusion in the text. For example, in Matthew 1:18 he helps us to understand Joseph's confusion over Mary's pregnancy: "Before they came to the marriage bed, Joseph discovered she was pregnant. (It was by the Holy Spirit, but he didn't know that.)" In Matthew 2:10 we are informed as to the reason for the excitement of the wise men upon their arrival in Bethlehem: "They could hardly contain themselves: they were in the right place! They had arrived at the right time!" These words are a considerable embellishment upon the NIV's "When they saw the star, they were overjoyed."

Peterson's use of idiomatic "street language" sometimes seems a bit forced. In Matthew 3:9, descendants of Abraham are described as being "neither here nor there." People say of Jesus in Luke 19:7 when he goes to the home of Zacchaeus, "What business does he have getting cozy with this crook?" And in John 8:45, the Jewish leaders say, "That clinches it."

Some renderings of particular verses are best described as simply strange. Consider the following paraphrases:

Romans 15:13—May the God of green hope fill you up with joy.

Romans 16:20—Enjoy the best of Jesus!

Galatians 6:13—All their talk about the law is gas.

The Message has filled a niche among Bible readers as a popular devotional Bible. And it is likely that this popularity will increase as people are attracted by its unorthodox appearance, unique style, and readability. But these very qualities make it unlikely that the paraphrase will ever become much more than an interesting curiosity in the world of Bible translations. The lack of verse numbers alone is sufficient reason for those readers who are looking for a Bible to use in group study and worship to leave this one at home.

Conclusion

This evaluation and analysis of dynamic translations and paraphrases brings us to the end of a journey that began in the ancient storytelling world of the Jewish people. We have covered a time span of thousands of years. And we have discovered that the concerns of those ancient storytellers are much like the concerns of Bible translators today. They must retell the stories of the Bible in such a way that those stories remain timeless enough to meet the spiritual needs of our own day. The task is not easy.

But this is only one stage in the process. Now the burden falls upon those of us who read these translations and paraphrases. In reading the Bible we become part of the grand story that it tells. For this reason, we now turn our attention to the task of choosing and using the Bible.

Suggested Readings

Bailey, Lloyd R., ed. *The Word of God: A Guide to English Versions of the Bible*. Atlanta: John Knox, 1982.

Kubo, Sakae, and Walter Specht. *So Many Versions? Twentieth-Century English Versions of the Bible*. Grand Rapids: Zondervan, 1975.

CHAPTER 5

Choosing—and Using—
a Translation:
Questions and Suggestions

L et's return to the opening scene of this book, in which the
young man and the salesclerk faced a bewildering array of
Bibles and translations. By now we hope that the books on that
shelf have become a little more familiar to you. But the young man's
problem remains the same: Which Bible should he choose?

In the first four chapters we talked about the history and development of the canon and the philosophies of translation that support
modern English translations. We evaluated the major verbal and
dynamic translations and paraphrases. Along the way we also over-
heard questions and comments such as: "It's all 'Greek' to me!";
"Why is my Bible different from yours?"; "Why does my translation
use such modern language?" We have tried to answer those questions, and others like them, in the first four chapters, but we always
come back to having to make a decision.

This chapter is about making that decision. What Bible do we
choose? How do we go about deciding? What do we do with that
Bible (or those Bibles) once we have it? This chapter is divided into
two sections. The first talks about the process of choosing a translation. The second addresses the ways in which we use that Bible. Each
of these sections is further divided into a set of questions and a set
of suggestions. The appendix that follows contains an annotated
bibliography of the translations and versions that are most readily
available. It is organized by year and should provide a quick and easy
reference.

Choosing a Translation

We hope you weren't expecting us to tell you which Bible is the "best" or the "right" translation. Actually, no single translation can claim to be the "best." Because so many excellent translations and versions of the Bible are available, such a choice must take into account individual preference as well as the relative strengths and weaknesses of each version. With that in mind, we offer the following questions to assist you as you make your choice.

Who Will Be Using the Bible?

Answering this question is very important. Bible translation and publishing is big business, and translations have become more specialized in order to attract a certain portion of the market. A Bible must "fit" the person, just as clothes must fit. This can be frustrating, especially if you are choosing a Bible for someone else. Since Bible sales have now exceeded $400 million annually, we suspect that a good many frustrated shoppers go through this exasperating process each year. One way to reduce the frustration is to consider the *vocabulary, biblical literacy,* and *theological knowledge or sophistication* of the person for whom you are selecting the Bible.

Many of the modern dynamic versions are designed to make the Bible accessible to those whose English vocabulary is limited or who are unfamiliar with the "biblical" vocabulary. Such versions are often excellent starting points for people who need a more accessible Bible. Biblical literacy and theological sophistication also play a role in answering this question. Those of an older generation (roughly over the ages of 40 to 45), as a group, are more familiar with the Bible and its stories, and they are also more comfortable with the concepts present in traditional biblical language. A dynamic translation may be stimulating for such people, but a more verbal version may serve their basic needs better.

Remember, there is no *one* set of *correct* answers to this question. Each person is different; the goal is to make sure that the Bible fits as well as possible.

How Will the Bible Be Used?

This may seem to be a silly question. For much of its history, the Bible was only available in a few formats. Therefore, the same Bible was used for private reading and study, public reading, and record keeping. Today, however, we should think about versions of the Bible in the same way we think of clothes. Most of us own more than one set of clothes. We wear certain clothes for playing and other clothes for working. Sometimes we dress "up"; other times we dress "down." Some clothes are more versatile than others, and we can wear them in a number of different contexts. The same is true for Bibles, particularly in this era of specialization. Just as the Bible must "fit" the person for whom it is purchased, it must also be appropriate to the use for which it is intended.

The first consideration is whether this Bible will be the only (or the main) Bible used. If so, it should be useful for public and private reading as well as for study. This broad range of uses would suggest any one of the verbal translations, with the exception of the NASB. One of the dynamic translations might be appropriate for this use, but considerable care should be taken in choosing a dynamic translation for such a wide range of uses.

If this version will serve as one among multiple versions, then questions about specific uses should be considered. For public reading and study, the verbal translations will be more suitable. For private reading and study, particularly when combined with a verbal translation, the dynamic translations may be more helpful. Anyone who is intent on doing serious Bible study, and who is unfamiliar with the ancient languages, should strongly consider using the NASB or its updated version. This is the only version firmly committed to preserving both the word order of the original texts and a verbal equivalence. While this philosophy makes the version difficult to read in public, it has no modern-language equal as a tool for private study.

A verbal translation is preferred for public reading. If such reading will occur on a regular basis, care should also be taken to choose a verbal translation that pays careful attention to the rhythm and style of the English language.

What Format Is the Most Useful?

This question, unfortunately, is where most people begin. In fact, many never get beyond this question to give attention to the more important questions mentioned above. In this era of intense competition for Bible sales, much of the energy of publishers has been spent on developing and marketing attractive formats. Regrettably, many retail clerks are no more knowledgeable about the various translations than their customers. Their response is often dictated by the advertising strategies of the publishers. As a result, many people choose a Bible for its format (binding, commentary or notes, translation helps, introductions, concordances, and the like), instead of for the usefulness of the translation itself.

Ask this question as a part of the process of choosing a translation. But ask it only after finding answers to the first two questions. Study Bibles and specialty Bibles will often be available in various translations. Choose a translation based on its own merits and usefulness, rather than because it comes in the preferred format.

We do not wish to suggest that format questions are unimportant. Many of the notes, introductions, and other helps that are packaged in Bible formats enhance the usefulness of the translation itself. Often, these additions are particularly useful because they are designed for specific situations and audiences. Some formats, such as those with a leather binding, for example, may lend a special air of sacredness to the Bible, reminding its reader that this volume is not just another book on the shelf. Other features, such as a binding in cloth or paperback, may increase the reader's level of comfort with the book itself, allowing the reader to make full use of the ideas and words of the Bible. One note of caution needs to be sounded, though, and we will return to it at various times in this chapter. Many publishers have combined the biblical text with the study or devotional notes of well-known ministers or authors. Consequently, the volumes take advantage of the popularity and name recognition of the commentator to sell the Bible in a particular format. Such a format may be that of a study Bible or of a devotional Bible, both of which can be very useful and highly informative. They may also be biased or prone to errors of fact and interpretation. For this reason, these Bibles need to be examined carefully before they are selected.

After answering these questions, you are ready to begin the process of choosing a translation. We offer the following suggestions to help you through that process.

Do Your Homework First

Selecting a Bible is much like making any other choice. In reality, though, most people devote considerably less time and effort to choosing a Bible than they should. We know people who spend weeks researching and comparing products before they buy any-thing, even a small appliance. They search through magazines, consult *Consumer Reports*, seek the advice of friends, and comparison shop before actually making a purchase. But they spend less than thirty minutes choosing a Bible.

The process of choosing a tool as important as the Bible *ought* to take a bit more time and thought. Reading our book is a good start. We recommend that you read other similar books, as well. Become well informed about the differences between modern versions *before* you start asking questions of trusted friends or salesclerks.

Make an Informed Decision

Doing your homework is merely the beginning. Use the infor-mation discovered in your research and reading. When you choose a translation, you need to be fully aware of the strengths and weak-nesses of each version. Which ancient text lies behind this modern translation? How accurate is the translation? What is the quality of the English language and syntax used?

Decide on the Format

We reserved this piece of advice for last. One of the unfortunate results of the marketing of the Bible is that many people select a version based on the format in which it is packaged rather than on the strengths of the version itself. New-car buyers are often advised not to "fall in love" with a particular car on the lot. The same car is available in a different color, with different options, or at another dealership for a lower price. While it may seem crass to compare purchasing a Bible to purchasing a car, the fact remains that your favorite translation is probably available in your favorite format. Selecting a version before deciding on the format will ensure that your Bible will be a cherished part of your life for many years.

Using a Translation

Like any other book or tool, ownership is not enough. We buy books to read; we buy tools to use. Either way one chooses to look at the Bible (book or tool), having one (or a dozen) sitting on the bookshelf is no guarantee of success. Success comes when the book is read to the reader's advantage; or, when the tool is chosen, meets the challenge, and enables completion of the task.

We have provided information about the Bible, its history, its translation into English, and its various versions. In this chapter, we have offered some specific advice on how to choose a translation or version. Such information is helpful only when it enables this new Bible to enhance your faith and life. Therefore, in this section of the chapter, we have some more questions and helpful suggestions as you use the Bible.

What Are You Trying to Accomplish?

This question is as important to the process of using a translation as it is to choosing one. Are you reading the Bible as part of an ongoing reading program? If so, you will probably be paying more attention to the broad outlines of stories and letters. Are you preparing a sermon, a Bible study, or a Sunday school lesson? If so, you will most likely be paying careful attention to details within significantly smaller passages. You also will probably be comparing a number of different translations of the same text.

The important thing is to ask the question first and be aware of your answer before you ever begin the task. Deliberate planning will make your use of the Bible more enjoyable and helpful.

How Familiar Are You with the Bible?

This question becomes more important to ask and answer with every new generation of Bible readers and churchgoers. Early in this century, such a question would have been answered quickly and with a great deal of certainty. Most people would not only have been familiar with the Bible and its stories and teachings, they would have been living in a world permeated by the Bible, its language, and its ideas. The development of technology and the proliferation of information have forced the Bible to compete for a place in our culture. An explosion of literacy, accompanied by an explosion of published literature, has pushed Bible reading into very specific territory. Few of us read or study the Bible outside of a religious context, and the number of Christians who are willing to do even that continues to dwindle. Churches have spent the last half of this century fighting over the Bible, or using the Bible to support their conflicting theological positions. In the process, the Bible has lost its central place even within the walls of the church.

Biblical literacy has become a problem. For the most part, those of us under the age of forty know significantly less about the Bible and its contents than do our older counterparts. The Bible has become just another book in our library, and we do not expend the effort or take the time to become proficient in its use. To a certain extent, this neglect of the Bible parallels our attitude toward Christianity and society as a whole. We search for easy answers and simple solutions. Our lives are so busy and cluttered that anything that demands time and energy to use is pushed to the margins of our existence.

If nothing else, the differences between an ancient culture and our modern one demand that we become familiar with both contexts in order to understand and apply the biblical revelation. Some of you may already be very familiar with the ancient world or may know where to find useful information about it that will help you understand the Bible. Others may need to work more diligently in order to make full use of the Bible in study and reading. Your level of biblical literacy is not nearly as important as being honest with yourself about where you stand. What will you need to know or find out in order to read and understand this passage? Do you know where you can go to get this information?

The wide range of biblical translations and formats actually becomes an advantage in finding a version that offers the most help for each particular level of biblical literacy. Comparing versions and their notes may also be a useful procedure as you use the Bible. However you choose to become biblically literate (or more literate), you should always be aware not only of what you know but of what you still need to learn as you read and study the Bible.

What Stands Between You and Your Use of the Bible?

The Bible no longer stands at the cultural center of our world. The barriers to reading the Bible that we face in the late twentieth century are much different from the barriers faced by our Christian ancestors. For centuries, reading the Bible was the privilege of those who were wealthy enough to own a copy or who were professional ministers. The Protestant Reformation and the invention of the printing press began to eliminate that privilege by making the Bible more readily accessible to anyone who desired to read it. Today, the Bible is available to almost everyone. It would seem that many of the barriers to reading the Bible have been eliminated.

Unfortunately, other barriers have taken the place of those traditional barriers of wealth and ordination. Time, or the lack of it, is a significant barrier. Although we have more free time than did previous generations, we also have more distractions. Daily newspapers, network news, and cable news channels have replaced the weekly newspaper or daily radio broadcast of the earlier era. Telephones, pagers, and computers render us instantly accessible at almost any time of day. We must even set aside time to "work out" because we no longer receive adequate exercise in the course of a normal workday. Even church, which used to demand our attention only when we could leave the farm to come into town, now attempts to program other available "free" time.

The abundance of information is also a barrier to reading the Bible. We live in a society suffering from information overload. Events from all around the world are instantly accessible to us in the privacy and comfort of our homes. Books, music, television, radio, and the Internet bombard us with information, sights, and sounds. With all this multisensory information to capture our attention, how can reading the Bible compete?

Finally, the desire for new and modern things also provides a barrier to the reading of the Bible. We want new clothes, new fashions, new cars, new information, new heroes, new leaders—the list quickly becomes overwhelming. Bible publishers make a valiant attempt to make the Bible attractive to a culture that is concerned only with the present, but most readers are quickly aware that the translation, no matter how modern, is still a translation of an ancient text. Once the ancient world becomes apparent, the Bible may lose its immediate relevance and be set aside in favor of something more recent and "in touch" with the modern world.

Reading the Bible and other spiritual exercises require as much diligence and intentionality as physical exercise. In a world full of distractions and barriers, we must make a conscious decision to develop the habit of reading and studying the Bible. An important part of making that decision involves understanding and removing the barriers that prevent us from coming to the Bible. We assume you have chosen a Bible because you are actually planning to use it. We hope that you will. Now we offer six suggestions for gaining the most benefit from using the Bible.

1. Find a Way to Live in the Context of the Bible

To use the Bible effectively, it is important to find a way to make the Bible and its message not only relevant to our lives, but central to our living. Most of the available strategies for increasing one's time with the Bible are products of a modern drive toward efficiency. Christians, it is argued, will be more effective spiritually if they are familiar with the Bible. The way to accomplish that goal is to involve every Christian in a program of Bible reading and study. This program should be a model of efficiency, imparting the most information in the least amount of time. In addition, Bible reading should be a part of an intense time of study and prayer colloquially known as a "quiet time," and we have used modern images to convince everyone that such a program is necessary. It has even been referred to as spiritual "fuel" or "gasoline."

With such emphasis on efficiency, Bible reading, prayer, and meditation have become means to an end, rather than ends in themselves. To borrow an image from the world of computers, we have approached reading and studying the Bible as a task to be opened in a "window" on the computer screen of our lives. Just as we might click on the "fixing dinner" icon, the "mowing the lawn" icon, the "going to work" icon, or the "driving the car pool" icon, we might also click on the "spiritual development" or "quiet time" icon. Then, we efficiently juggle the tasks, switching back and forth between them. For those readers who are unfamiliar with computers, a "to-do" list serves as an equally good analogy. We have a variety of tasks on such a list, which we check off as we complete them. Such an approach assumes the Bible is no more important to our daily living than the newspaper or situation comedy that also occupies a slot in our calendars.

Living out of the context of the Bible will demand more than an efficient, modern approach to the Bible. We need to consider the Bible and Christianity to be the "operating system," which remains active as long as the computer is in use. Sometimes it lies unseen and unnoticed in the background, but it is always only a keystroke or mouse-click away.

To put it another way, the truth of the Bible rests in its ability to transform the lives of its readers. But this can only happen when we immerse ourselves so completely in its pages that it becomes the very foundation from which we live out the faith. As we read the stories of the Bible we ask a simple question: How should I live in light of these stories? In this way, the stories themselves shape our "to-do" list, rather than being another item on it.

2. Do Not Confuse Commentary or Notes with the Bible Itself

As we mentioned above, the packaging of commentary or study notes with the biblical text has created a problem that previous generations of readers did not face. Often these notes have become the focus of a marketing or advertising plan, and this raises even more questions about the integrity of the translation or version being used. We are not arguing here for the removal of such notes; they can be quite helpful in understanding difficult passages. Such formats run a considerable risk, though, that the reader will not distinguish between the notes and the text itself. Subconsciously, the reader may give the notes or commentary an authority equal to that of the Bible.

In a perfect world, this might not present a problem. With the profusion of different versions and formats, however, publishers have adopted a "buyer beware" stance. Anyone with the financial resources can (and often does) publish a biblical translation and commentary. Modern technology allows publishers to integrate text, commentary, notes, and graphics almost seamlessly. While we might be wary of such notes and commentary when they are published in a separate volume, their presence alongside the Bible encourages us to regard them with much more confidence and trust.

Jesus cautioned his followers to be "sensible as serpents and free of guile as doves" (Matthew 10:16). This situation would seem to be one that requires the full use of our sensibility. Everyone probably ought to have at least one Bible that has as few interpretative notes as possible. Reading this version would allow one to experience the text first, before encountering commentary and explanation. Second, as we mentioned in the section above on choosing a Bible, when you select a Bible, take considerable care to evaluate the quality and theological biases of the notes that are a part of the format. Finally, you ought also to consult notes and commentary from sources other than your study or devotional Bible. This will remind you that other ways of reading this particular passage also exist, and that your understanding of the passage will be enriched by such comparison.

3. Move Beyond Chapter and Verse Divisions

People seem surprised to discover that the chapter and verse divisions were not part of the original text of the Bible. In fact, they are a relatively recent addition to the text. Such divisions were unimportant before the publication of a variety of different versions. When the only available versions were in Latin (or the ancient languages) and the only people who read the Bible were priests or scholars, passages were identified by key words or phrases since everyone was familiar with the language of the translation. For the laypeople of the church, often unable to read, the Scriptures were encountered through the liturgy (or worship service) of the church. They had either memorized these portions of the lectionary, or the priest prompted them to repeat the words of Scripture as the worship service proceeded. With the increasing availability of the Bible came a need for a more standard point of reference. Therefore, chapter and verse divisions were introduced to allow persons using different translations or versions to have a common reference point for reading the same passage.

Unfortunately, such divisions can inhibit the reading and comprehension of the biblical text. Few other pieces of literature have such an intrusive system of reference, and the divisions cannot help but influence our reading of the Bible. We insist on reading short passages (sometimes no more than one verse) in the context of worship. Congregations begin to squirm and shift in their seats during the reading of a lengthy passage. We are in danger of creating generations of worshipers and Bible readers who have experienced the Bible only in fragments—and very small fragments at that. We read the Bible the way students read textbooks—one chapter at a time—and then only the minimum needed to complete the "assignment."

If the Bible is to become central to the Christian's life, then we must attempt to recover a reading of the texts that gives attention to their nature as sacred *literature*. Therefore, Paul's Letters need to be read as letters, not just as disjointed theological statements. The

Gospels tell a story with a beginning, middle, and end; we need to read those stories in their entirety, not just piecemeal. Psalms need to be sung; poetry needs to be recited. We must recover a sense of the dramatic force of the biblical text to allow it to live and breathe life into its readers.

4. Use More Than One Version

Much of the anxiety involved in choosing a particular version will disappear if you are willing and able to use more than one version, particularly in the context of study. The availability of so many versions becomes an advantage when one no longer must rely on just one translation and its interpretation of the ancient texts.

We recommend that you use at least three versions. One should be a verbal translation; the other two could be dynamic translations, perhaps with different levels of fidelity to the words and order of the ancient Greek and Hebrew. The process of reading and comparing the translations in this way will enrich your understanding of the text and aid you in hearing nuances of meaning that may be obscured in the translation process. Should you be limited to one translation, however, we strongly suggest using a verbal translation with as little interpretative bias as possible.

5. Be Aware of Differences Between Versions and the Nature of Those Differences

This suggestion is closely related to the preceding one. An awareness of the differences between versions—and the reasons for those differences—will help you know how best to use each version in tandem with the others. Not all differences are matters of interpretation. Sometimes versions vary because they have chosen to translate a different ancient text. Other differences may be the result of choosing between interpretative options. Still others may result from translation philosophy or English stylistic preferences. Whatever the reasons for the difference, your awareness is important to using the Bible to its fullest.

An awareness of differences will also remind you not to be searching perpetually for the "right" or "best" version. Fight the urge to find the one version that will serve all your needs equally well. The version that is right for you is the one that best serves your purpose at the point of use. No serious mechanic would try to repair a complicated piece of machinery with only a pair of pliers. A full complement of tools is necessary for the successful completion of such a job. In the same way, serious scholars of the Bible (and we assume that all Christians ought to be serious students of the Bible) need a broad range of tools at their disposal in order to read and understand the Scriptures, which ought to lie at the center of their lives.

6. Become as Familiar as Possible with the World of the Bible

One of the inescapable realities of translating the Bible from the ancient languages into any modern language is the necessity to interpret. Many words have more than one meaning, and combining those words increases the range of possible meanings. Therefore, even a translation that uses a word-for-word verbal philosophy will require some interpretation in order to make the transition from the ancient to the modern world. In addition, the Bible remains an ancient book, full of ancient stories that occurred in an ancient world. Not only does the process of translation demand interpretation, the process of reading will require you to interpret the ancient text in its context.

This is not an unfamiliar task to most of us. The act of reading itself demands an ability to interpret what is written within its context. For example, understanding the sentence "I read the paper" involves deciding whether the act is taking place now or has already been completed; this is determined by understanding the context of the sentence. Those who read historical fiction or biographies, even those who watch films set in other locations or historical settings, are constantly interpreting and determining context.

What sets reading and studying the Bible apart from other books is that the Bible is immediately recognizable as ancient literature. The world of the Bible is unfamiliar in our modern context. It is a world without technology, without mass communication, even without Americans! And the stories, written as they were for ancient audiences, have retained their ancient flavor. Explanatory notes can help us visualize the modern equivalents of ancient objects and places, but we must also study the culture and history that pervade the world of the Bible.

Many readers of the Bible are unwilling to give the required time and effort. To them, the Bible ought to be immediately and fully comprehensible. As biblical literacy continues to decline, this attitude will increase. Yet, some stories only come to life when one understands ancient Mediterranean culture. Others only make sense in the light of the histories of Israel, Egypt, and Greece. Most of the stories in the Bible will be confusing unless the reader has some knowledge of the geography of that world. Understanding and reading the Bible will demand the sophistication of a lifetime of study.

Tremendous strides have been made in the past fifty years toward our understanding of the ancient Mediterranean world. During that same time, equally important attempts have been made to ensure that such information is available to anyone who can read or use a computer to learn about those discoveries. A flood of books and magazine articles, complete with pictures, has brought the ancient world into our libraries, our classrooms, even our living rooms. There is little excuse for not knowing about the world of the Bible.

If you hope to use the Bible successfully, you must be prepared to learn and study, not just the Bible itself, but the world from which the Bible emerged. Only then will the stories and people of its pages come to life, to have their words and actions translated into the pages of your life.

Conclusion

We hope that the information in these pages is useful, enlightening, and—dare we say it—even inspiring. Choosing a Bible can be a wonderful journey of discovery. But take care to avoid the pitfalls. Remember that no single translation is the best, or even the most correct, among all of the modern English translations. Do not become so dazed by the range of choices that you are unable to choose.

In the end, though, the decision is yours. But in this era of new and newer versions the choice need not be final. You will have a chance to choose again and again. In fact, we recommend owning more than one version. Now we offer a challenge: commit yourself not only to choosing a Bible, but to using it. Any book that we affirm as "Scripture" ought to be read with joy, abandon, and reverence.

After all, this book contains the words of Torah, the writings of the prophets and holy ones of Israel, the stories of the life of Jesus, and the words of his disciples. As so many before us have done, we commend them to you.

Suggested Readings

Adam, A. K. M. *What is Postmodern Biblical Criticism?* Minneapolis: Augsburg Fortress, 1995.

Malina, Bruce J. *The New Testament World: Insights from Cultural Anthropology.* Atlanta: John Knox, 1981.

Miller, Max. *The History of Israel: An Essential Guide.* Nashville: Abingdon, 1998.

Nash, Robert N., Jr. *An 8-Track Church in a CD World: The Modern Church in the Postmodern World.* Macon: Smyth & Helwys, 1997.

APPENDIX

An Annotated Bibliography of Selected Versions

Print Versions

1901

American Standard Version. Nashville: Thomas Nelson and Son. Verbal equivalence. An American revision of the King James Version.

1902

The Twentieth-Century New Testament. New York: Fleming H. Revell Co. Dynamic equivalence. An early attempt to make the Bible intelligible to modern readers, especially children.

1903

Weymouth, Richard Francis. The New Testament in Modern Speech: An Idiomatic Translation into Every Day English from the text of the Resultant Greek Testament. New York: Baker and Taylor. Revised in 1924 and 1929. Dynamic equivalence. Weymouth was one of the translators for The Twentieth-Century New Testament, and his translation is based on his own edition of the Greek New Testament.

1907

Moulton, Richard G. Moulton's Modern Reader's Bible. New York: Macmillan. Dynamic equivalence.

1917

The Holy Scriptures According to the Masoretic Text: A New Translation with the Aid of Previous Versions and with Constant

Consultation of Jewish Authorities. Philadelphia: The Jewish Publication Society. Verbal equivalence. Little more than a revision of the KJV in 1917, the New Jewish Version was a thorough revision and translation completed in 1955.

1924

Montgomery, Helen B. The Centenary Translation of the New Testament in Modern English. Philadelphia: Judson Press. Dynamic equivalence. An excellent translation to commemorate the one hundredth anniversary of the American Baptist Publication Society.

1926

Moffatt, James. A New Translation of the Bible. New York and London: Harper and Brothers. Dynamic equivalence. A very influential early translation by a reputable Scottish scholar.

1927

Smith, J. M. Powis, and Edgar Goodspeed, eds. The Bible—An American Translation. Chicago: University of Chicago Press. Dynamic equivalence. A well-respected modern language version, one of the first to eliminate "thee" and "thou" from the New Testament.

1937

Williams, Charles B. The New Testament: A Translation in the Language of the People. Boston: Bruce Humphries. Revised edition published in 1950 by Moody Press. Dynamic equivalence. An attempt to translate the New Testament into practical, everyday language. Williams also endeavored to translate the Greek tenses as accurately as possible. The two aims are sometimes in tension.

1945

Knox, Ronald A. The New Testament in English. London: Burns and Oates. Dynamic equivalence. A Roman Catholic version, translated from the Latin Vulgate. The Old Testament was published in 1949; the entire Bible was published in 1955.

Verkuyl, Gerrit. Berkeley Version of the New Testament. Berkeley: James J. Gillick and Co. Dynamic equivalence. The precursor to the Modern Language Bible, published in 1959 by Zondervan.

1952

Revised Standard Version. New York, Toronto, and Edinburgh: Thomas Nelson and Sons. Verbal equivalence. An excellent translation from the ancient languages, intended to update the KJV for study and worship.

1957

Lamsa, George M. The Holy Bible from Ancient Eastern Manuscripts. Philadelphia: A. J. Holman Co. Dynamic equivalence. Translated from the Peshitta, a version in Syriac (rather than Aramaic as Lamsa claimed).

1958

Phillips, J. B. The New Testament in Modern English. New York: Macmillan. Dynamic equivalence. Perhaps the best-known individual translation of the New Testament, Phillips provided this translation for the young people of his postwar London parish. He was encouraged by C. S. Lewis.

1961

New World Translation of the Holy Scriptures. New World Bible Translation Committee. Brooklyn: Watchtower Bible and Tract Society of New York. Verbal equivalence. The translation of the Jehovah's Witnesses. This version has a tendency toward theological and interpretative bias.

1965

The Amplified Bible. Grand Rapids: Zondervan. Verbal equivalence. This is based on an acceptable translation, but its contribution lies in the ability to explore a range of meanings for each word. In this, it tends to function as a commentary rather than a translation.

1966

Jerusalem Bible. Garden City, N.J.: Doubleday. Dynamic equivalence. A translation from the French, La Sainte Bible. This translation is known for its literary quality, but also shows a tendency to emend the text, often without good reason.

1968

Jordan, Clarence. The Cotton Patch Version. New York: Association Press. Dynamic equivalence. Jordan was the founder of the Koinonia Community in Americus, Georgia, an interracial farming community. This version sets the New Testament in the American South and uses a local dialect rather than standard

Key's Broadway show brought this version to national prominence.

1970

The New American Bible. New York: P. J. Kennedy. Verbal equivalence. A competent version intended for an American Roman Catholic audience.

The New English Bible with the Apocrypha. Oxford: Cambridge University Press. Dynamic equivalence. An English version, intentionally outside of the KJV tradition. The translation committee showed a tendency to develop their own text and include interpretative comments. The language of this translation does have a certain style and is certainly formal enough to be used in public worship.

1971

New American Standard Bible. La Habra, Calif.: Lockman Foundation. Verbal equivalence. Committed to a literal translation of the ancient languages, even reproducing the ancient word order. Excellent for study purposes but too stilted for public worship.

The Living Bible. Wheaton, Il.: Tyndale House. Paraphrase. Produced by Kenneth Taylor, the LB became overwhelmingly popular. Unlike many other modern versions, its conservatism appealed to those who were still reading the KJV, but wanted a version they could understand with more ease.

1973

The New International Version. Grand Rapids: Zondervan. Verbal equivalence (with considerable freedom). Perhaps the best-selling modern version, probably because it has been advertised as a conservative evangelical translation. Particularly useful for public reading, but it has some significant theological biases.

1976

Good News for Modern Man: Today's English Version. New York: American Bible Society. Dynamic equivalence-Common language. One of the first committee-produced versions to advocate the philosophy of dynamic equivalence. New Testament (1966).

1979

The New King James Version. Nashville: Thomas Nelson. Verbal equivalence. An update of the KJV, it offers little more than some more modern words. It has not, and should not have, replaced the KJV.

1982

The Reader's Digest Bible. New York: Random House. Verbal equivalence. A condensation of the RSV, this version generated a considerable amount of publicity.

1985

New Jerusalem Bible. Garden City, N.J.: Doubleday. Verbal equivalence. A revision of the JB, this version represents a shift in translation philosophy for the family of versions. It also addresses the question of inclusive language, although in a rather conservative fashion. Available in both a study edition (with excellent notes) and a reader's edition.

1989

The New Revised Standard Version. New York: Division of Christian Education of the National Council of Churches. Verbal equivalence. A long-awaited revision of the RSV, the NRSV addresses the question of inclusive language and provides a new translation from the ancient languages. The basis for reputable study bibles such as the Oxford Annotated Bible and the HarperCollins Study Bible.

Revised English Bible with Apocrypha. Cambridge: Cambridge University Press. Dynamic equivalence. A revision of the NEB, the REB provides a much more readable version. It has been criticized for a rather sporadic attempt to use inclusive language.

1991

New Century Version. Waco, TX: Word. Dynamic equivalence. The successor to the International Children's Bible, the NCV is clear, readable, and uses inclusive language.

1993

Peterson, Eugene H. *The Message: The New Testament in Contemporary Language*. Colorado Springs: NavPress. Paraphrase. A popular version produced by a Presbyterian pastor. Intended to retain the informal character of New Testament Greek in the modern English translation. A good translation, often marred by a tendency to add interpretative comments.

1994

The 21st Century King James Version. Gary, S.D.: Deuel Enterprises. Verbal equivalence. The project of William Prindele, who attempted to compare the 1611 KJV with *Webster's International Dictionary, Second Edition Unabridged* in order to produce a modernized version of the KJV.

1995

The Contemporary English Version. New York: American Bible Society. Dynamic equivalence–Common language. The dynamic equivalence philosophy of translation that produced the GNB/TEV virtually guaranteed a successor such as the CEV. The English language had changed sufficiently in almost twenty years to warrant a new translation. The CEV gives particular attention to the sound of the text, attempting to eliminate the rhythm and cadence of the Hebrew and Greek from the modern English of the translation.

New American Standard Bible, Updated. La Habra, Calif.: Lockman Foundation. Verbal equivalence. More modern language than its parent and an attempt to make the translation more fluid than the NASB. Still too stilted for public worship, but some of the features continue to recommend this version as useful for study.

New International Reader's Version. Grand Rapids: Zondervan. Verbal equivalence. The NirV is a revision of the NIV, designed to be accessible to those who read at or below the fourth-grade level.

New Testament and Psalms: An Inclusive Version. New York: Oxford. Verbal equivalence (with a good deal of freedom). A revision of the NRSV with the stated purpose of making its language gender-inclusive. Dubbed the "PC" Bible, it generated a good deal of publicity.

1996

New Living Translation. Wheaton, Il.: Tyndale House. Dynamic equivalence. In the tradition of the LB, but a new translation from the ancient languages. Conservative evangelical in theology.

Electronic Resources

Study Editions

Accordance. Gramcord Institute. Macintosh. Powerful Bible study program including ancient language texts and English Bible versions.

Bible/Master. Lockman Foundation. Windows or Macintosh. Primarily developed in order to allow electronic access to the NASB, it also contains the NASB Update, the NIV, and the KJV. It is fairly simple to use, although not as sophisticated as Gramcord/Bible Companion or Logos.

Bible Windows. Silver Mountain Software. Windows. Can perform grammatical searches in both Greek and Hebrew. Somewhat limited collection of reference works, but good value for the relatively low cost.

Bible Works for Windows. Hermeneutika Software. Windows. Fairly powerful grammatical searches, though not as advanced as *Gramcord*. English and non-English versions available.

Gramcord for Windows/Bible Companion. Gramcord Institute/White Harvest. Windows. Excellent product, especially if one is interested in grammatical searches and scholarly resources. Good value.

Logos Bible Study Software. Logos Research Systems. Windows. Excellent collection of reference books. Available in four different levels and easy to use. Highest level is somewhat expensive.

PC Study Bible. Biblesoft. Windows. Relatively inexpensive with a small number of reference works and a capable search engine. Contains no ancient language texts.

QuickVerse. Parsons Technology. Windows. For the user with no need for ancient language texts, this is perhaps the easiest and most popular way to access the Bible electronically.

The Word Advanced Study System. WordSoft/Word. DOS/GUI. Includes basic texts and helps. Somewhat clumsy to use but has powerful grammatical and word search capabilities.

WORDsearch. NavPress. Windows. Easy to learn and contains many of the most popular English translations. Also includes helpful Bible study tools.

Bibles and Tools

HyperBible. Kirkbride Technology. Windows or Macintosh. Based on the Thompson Chain Reference Bible with the KJV, NASB, NIV, NKJV, RSV, and LB available. Also includes some other helps, including a pronunciation feature.

IVP Study Bible. InterVarsity Press. Windows. Includes NRSV, REB, AV and *IVP New Bible Commentary*, *IVP New Bible Dictionary*, and *IVP New Bible Atlas*. Compatible with Lion PC Bible Handbook.

Lion PC Bible Handbook. Lion Publishing. Windows. Includes NIV and other resources from Lion Publishing.

The New Oxford Annotated Bible, New Revised Standard Version. Oxford. Windows. For those who fell in love with the Oxford Annotated Bible, an electronic version. Digitally linked to the *Oxford Companion to the Bible* and *Oxford Bible Maps*. All three are available as The New Oxford Annotated Biblical Reference Library. Probably the best product that only provides access to a Bible version.